D1569208

Contrapunctus

Prosdocimo de' Beldomandi, professor of arts and medicine at Padua in the early fifteenth century, brought to his eight treatises on music an originality, a scientific rigor, and an aesthetic sensitivity that made him one of the preeminent music theorists of his time. In the *Contrapunctus* (1412) he surveyed the practice of counterpoint and musica ficta, codifying each in six rules. Unlike most of his contemporaries, who were satisfied merely to state their rules, Prosdocimo justified his, making the treatise a primer of the musical aesthetics of his time.

A critical edition and translation are long overdue. The only available edition, that of Coussemaker (1869), is a faulty transcription of a single idiosyncratic source. Five sources survive, one of which preserves a revision that Prosdocimo prepared late in life, sharpening his definitions of the intervals, amplifying his rules of counterpoint, clarifying his rules of musica ficta (advocating, in fact, the ear as the final arbiter in such matters), and incorporating sharp reproofs of Marchetto, the unorthodox Paduan theorist of a century earlier.

The present edition is based on a collation of all five sources and includes an annotated translation on facing pages. A critical introduction places Prosdocimo and his treatise in their historical context, and indexes for terms, names, and subjects are included.

Jan Herlinger is an assistant professor of music at Duke University. He is the editor and translator of *The "Lucidarium" of Marchetto of Padua* and the author of articles in the *Journal of the American Musicological Society, Acta Musicologica,* and *Music Theory Spectrum.*

Greek and Latin Music Theory

Thomas J. Mathiesen,
General Editor
Brigham Young University

Jon Solomon,
Associate Editor
University of Arizona

Prosdocimo de' Beldomandi

CONTRAPUNCTUS

Counterpoint

A new critical text and
translation on facing pages,
with an introduction, annotations,
and *indices verborum*
and *nominum et rerum* by

Jan Herlinger

University of Nebraska Press
Lincoln and London

Manufactured in the
United States of America

The paper in this book meets the
guidelines for permanence and durability
of the Committee on Production Guidelines
for Book Longevity of the Council
on Library Resources

Library of Congress Cataloging in Publication Data
Prosdocimus, de Beldemandis, d. 1428.
[Contrapunctus. English & Latin]
Contrapunctus = Counterpoint.
(Greek and Latin music theory ; 1)
Includes indexes.
1. Counterpoint—15th century. I. Herlinger, Jan W.
II. Title. III. Title: Counterpoint. IV. Series
MT5.5.P7613 1984 781.4'2 83-23367
ISBN 0-8032-3669-7

To Tina

CONTENTS

SERIES EDITOR'S PREFACE ix

PREFACE xi

INTRODUCTION 1

Prosdocimo and His Treatises 1
The *Contrapunctus* 7
Prosdocimo's Place 13
The Manuscripts 14
The Edition 22

CONSPECTUS CODICUM ET NOTARUM 25

CONTRAPUNCTUS 26

Book 1 26
Book 2 28
Book 3 34
Book 4 58
Book 5 70

APPENDIX: PROSDOCIMO AND UGOLINO 97

INDEX VERBORUM 99

INDEX NOMINUM ET RERUM 107

SERIES EDITOR'S PREFACE

With this volume, we mark the inauguration of a new series, Greek and Latin Music Theory, and we are delighted to begin with the *Contrapunctus* of Prosdocimo de' Beldomandi, as introduced, edited, and translated by Jan Herlinger. Because our series intends to present Greek and Latin treatises ranging over the whole of music theory from the speculative to the technical to the practical, it is surely appropriate to begin with an author like Prosdocimo, whose own musical works represent this breadth of interest.

It is undoubtedly also appropriate in beginning a series to say something about the principles that will guide the volumes as they appear. Readers of our series will know from these principles what they may expect to find in each book and what the volume and series editors have set as their ideal.

The series aims to establish and publish truly critical texts for the many works of ancient and medieval music theory in Greek and Latin that do not presently exist in critical editions and to provide translations on facing pages with annotations illuminating the content of the treatise. Each volume will include a major introductory essay discussing, as appropriate, the significance of the treatise to its theoretical tradition; the life of its author (or, for anonymous works, the probable authors); the design, sources, and theoretical premises of the treatise; the manuscripts used to establish the text and the actual establishment of the text itself; *loci paralleli* and quotations; and special considerations involved in the translation. The texts will be based on a full collation of every relevant manuscript--insofar as possible--and the collation will be reported in a critical apparatus at the bottom of each text page. The text critical work will largely follow Martin L. West's *Textual Criticism and Editorial Technique Applicable to Greek and Latin Texts* (Stuttgart: Teubner, 1973). The translations are intended to be readable, but at the same time, they will attempt to preserve in large measure the consistency, variety, and subtlety of the original. Special care will be given to the treatment of technical vocabulary, syntactic subtleties, and consistency of terminology.

Finally, each volume will also include *indices verborum, nominum et rerum*.

The books in the series are prepared in camera-ready format by the various volume editors. Each book follows a style guide for the series that insures consistency from volume to volume.

It is a pleasure to acknowledge the encouragement and helpful advice the series has received from many quarters during its gestation. Special thanks must be extended to the advance reviewers of this volume and to the College of Fine Arts and Communications at Brigham Young University and its dean, James A. Mason, for generous grants in support of the series.

Thomas J. Mathiesen

General Editor,
Greek and Latin Music Theory

PREFACE

Prosdocimo de' Beldomandi, professor of arts and medicine at Padua in the early fifteenth century, brought to his eight treatises on music an originality, a scientific rigor, and an aesthetic sensitivity that made him one of the preeminent music theorists of his time. In the *Contrapunctus* (1412) he surveyed the practice of counterpoint and musica ficta, codifying each in six rules. Unlike most of his contemporaries, who were satisfied merely to state their rules, Prosdocimo justified his, thus making the treatise a primer of the musical aesthetics of his time.

A critical edition and translation are long overdue. The only available edition, that of Coussemaker (1869), is a faulty transcription of a single idiosyncratic source. Five sources survive, one of which preserves a revision that Prosdocimo prepared late in life, sharpening his definitions of the intervals, amplifying his rules of counterpoint, clarifying his rules of musica ficta (advocating, in fact, the ear as the final arbiter in such matters), and incorporating sharp reproofs of Marchetto, the unorthodox Paduan theorist of a century earlier.

Professor Edward E. Lowinsky, who had seen the Lucca manuscript that contains Prosocimo's revision of the *Contrapunctus* and had recognized its importance, presented a photographic copy of it to his seminar on musica ficta at the University of Chicago some fifteen years ago. I thank Professor Lowinsky most warmly for thus introducing me to Prosdocimo--and, indeed, to the music theory of the Middle Ages--and for his continued interest, support, and criticism.

Thanks are due also to Thomas J. Mathiesen for his careful reading of the text and his many thoughtful suggestions; to Helen Jenner of Chapel Hill, North Carolina, for the musical autography; and to two graduate research assistants at Duke University: Caroline Usher, for calligraphy and for preparing the *index verborum*; and Janet Best, for assistance with proofreading.

The financial assistance of the following is gratefully acknowledged: the National Endowment for the Humanities and the Duke University Research Council, for supporting research for the book; the Mary Duke Biddle Foundation, for supporting production of the volume.

INTRODUCTION

Prosdocimo and His Treatises

What is known of the life of Prosdocimo de' Beldomandi is quickly told. He was a student of arts in Padua in 1400 and in 1402, and he once called himself "Prosdocimus de Beldemandis of Padua, student of arts at Bologna." He took his doctorate in arts at Padua on 15 May 1409 and received the license in medicine there on 15 April 1411. During part of 1412 and 1413 he was at Montagnana, a fortified town some forty km southwest of Padua. On 26 July 1420 he was present at a convocation of doctors of the Sacred College of Arts and Medicine. He was a professor at Padua from 1422 at the latest until 1428, the year of his death. The documents list him as professor of astrology or astronomy, or among the lectors of "astrology, mathematics, and experimental philosophy" or "arts and medicine."[1]

---

[1]For references to Prosdocimo as a student at Padua, see Antonio Favaro, "Appendice agli studi intorno alla vita ed alle opere di Prosdocimo de' Beldomandi, matematico padovano del secolo XV," *Bullettino di bibliografia e di storia delle scienze matematiche e fisiche* 18 (1885):420; for Prosdocimo's reference to his study at Bologna, I-Fl, ms. Ashburnham 206, f. 19r, quoted in Favaro, "Appendice," p. 407, and F. Alberto Gallo, "La tradizione dei trattati musicali di Prosdocimo de Beldemandis," *Quadrivium* 6 (1964):58.

Prosdocimo wrote treatises 4, 5, 6, and 11 at Montagnana in 1412 and 1413.

On Prosdocimo's degrees, see Antonio Favaro, "Intorno alla vita ed alle opere di Prosdocimo de' Beldomandi, matematico padovano del secolo XV," *Bullettino di bibliografia e di storia delle scienze matematiche e fisiche* 12 (1879):22-23, and *Acta graduum academicorum gymnasii patavini*, ed. Gasparo Zonta and Giovanni Brotto (Padua: Typis Seminarii, 1922), pp. 4, 42-43 (nos. 31, 155). In Prosdoci-

Prosdocimo's musical treatises fall into three distinct groups. Three seem to date from his student years:

1. *Expositiones tractatus pratice cantus mensurabilis Johannis de Muris* (Padua, 1404 [?])
2. *Tractatus pratice cantus mensurabilis* (by 1409 [?])
3. *Brevis summula proportionum quantum ad musicam pertinet* (by 1409 [?]).

Four may be regarded as the central musical treatises of his maturity:

4. *Contrapunctus* (Montagnana, 1412)
5. *Tractatus pratice cantus mensurabilis ad modum Ytalicorum* (Montagnana, 1412)
6. *Tractatus plane musice* (Montagnana, 1412)
7. *Parvus tractatulus de modo monacordum dividendi* (Padua, 1413).

Late in life he wrote the treatise on speculative music that is, in substance, an attack on Marchetto of Padua:

8. *Tractatus musice speculative* (1425).[2]

---

mo's day, a private examination (*examen*) for the license to teach was prerequisite to the public examination (*conventus*) for the doctorate; see Nancy G. Siraisi, *Arts and Sciences at Padua: The Studium of Padua before 1350*, Studies and Texts, no. 25 (Toronto: Pontifical Institute of Mediaeval Studies, 1973), p. 31.

For the 1420 convocation and for various citations during the years 1422, 1424, 1427, and 1428, see Favaro, "Intorno," pp. 29-31, 34-38, and *Acta graduum academicorum gymnasii patavini*, pp. 153, 156 (nos. 658, 685, 693).

[2]All the treatises are attributed to Prosdocimo in one or more manuscripts.

Treatise 1, Prosdocimo's commentary on the *Libellus cantus mensurabilis* of Johannes de Muris, is dated 1404 in I-Bc, ms. A.56 (henceforward: B); 1412 in the only other source, I-CATc, ms. Ursino-Recupero D.39. B is the most reliable of the manuscripts that transmit Prosdocimo's musical treatises, D.39 generally unreliable; and it is probable that Prosdocimo would have commented on the standard mensural treatise of his time before undertaking his own work on the subject (treatise 2, below). The treatise has been published: *Expositiones tractatus pratice cantus mensurabilis magistri Johannis de Muris*, ed. F. Alberto Gallo, Antiqui musicae italicae scriptores, no.

In addition to the musical treatises, Prosdocimo wrote at least two on arithmetic:

9. *Canon in quo docetur modus componendi et operandi tabulam quandam* (Padua, 1409 [or 1419?])
10. *Algorismus de integris sive pratica arismetrice de integris* (Padua, 1410);

nine on astronomy:

11. *Brevis tractatulus de electionibus secundum situm lune in suis 28 mansionibus* (Montagnana, 1413)
12. *Scriptum super tractatu de spera Johannis de Sacrobosco* (Padua, 1418)

3: Prosdocimi de Beldemandis opera, vol. 1 (Bologna: Antiquae Musicae Italicae Studiosi, 1966).

Treatises 2 and 3 appear on ff. 77v-88r and 91r-92r of I-Fl, ms. Ashburnham 206. The statutes of the Paduan College of Artists and Physicians of 1409 appear on ff. 107v-110v. If Prosdocimo copied these statutes in connection with the completion of his studies, the treatises would presumably date from his student years. For other sources, see F. Alberto Gallo, "Trattati di Prosdocimo," p. 31. The treatises are published in *Scriptorum de musica medii aevi nova series a Gerbertina altera* (henceforward: CS), 4 vols., ed. Edmond de Coussemaker (Paris: Durand, 1864-1876), 3:200-28 and 258-61 respectively.

All manuscripts (see Gallo, "Trattati di Prosdocimo," pp. 31-32) agree on the date and place of composition of treatises 4, 5, 6, and 7. Treatise 4 appears on pp. 193-99, 5 on pp. 228-48, 7 on pp. 248-58 of CS 3. For an edition of Prosdocimo's revision of treatise 7, see Claudio Sartori, *La notazione italiana del Trecento in una redazione inedita del "Tractatus practice cantus mensurabilis ad modum ytalicorum" di Prosdocimo de Beldemandis* (Florence: Olschki, 1938), pp. 35-71, with an English translation, Prosdocimus de Beldemandis, *A Treatise on the Practice of Mensural Music in the Italian Manner*, trans. Jay A. Huff, Musicological Studies and Documents, no. 29 (N.p.: American Institute of Musicology, 1972).

The date and place of copying for treatise 8 appear in I-Lg, ms. 359 (henceforward: L); the only other source, B, lacks a colophon. For an edition, see D. Raffaello Baralli and Luigi Torri, "Il *Trattato* di Prosdocimo de' Beldomandi contro il *Lucidario* di Marchetto da Padova per la prima volta trascritto e illustrato," *Rivista musicale italiana* 20 (1913):731-62.

13. *Canones de motibus corporum supercelestium* (Padua, 1424)
14. *Tabule mediorum motuum, equationum, stationum et latitudinum planetarum, elevationis signorum, diversitatis aspectus lune, mediarum coniunctionum et oppositionum lunarium, feriarum, latitudinum climatum, longitudinum et latitudinum civitatum*
15. *Stelle fixe verificate tempore Alphonsi*
16. *Canon ad inveniendum tempus introitus solis in quodcumque 12 signorum in zodiaco*
17. *Canon ad inveniendum introitum lune in quodlibet signorum in zodiaco*
18. *Compositio astrolabii*
19. *Astrolabium*;

and one on geometry:

20. *De parallelogramo*.[3]

Prosdocimo's writings on music, arithmetic, and astronomy are those of an expert. His eight treatises on music constitute a systematic survey of the main departments of the art and show not only a comprehension of the authorities most influential in the academic circles of the day, Boethius and Johannes de Muris, but also a sense of the development of musical theory over the preceding hundred years or so: he knew, for instance, that

---

[3]For manuscript sources of the treatises on arithmetic, astronomy, and geometry, see Favaro, "Intorno," pp. 41-74, 115-221.

For treatise 9, B gives the date 1409; three other manuscripts give 1419. I have accepted the former because of the general reliability of B. The treatise was published by Favaro, "Intorno," pp. 143-45.

Treatise 10 was printed in Padua, 1483, and in Venice, 1540; the latter gives the date of composition as 1460, obviously impossible. The date 1410 comes from B.

Treatise 11 appears only in B, which gives the date.

Three of four manuscript sources for treatise 12 give the date 1418; the other has 1348, obviously impossible. It was printed in Venice, 1531.

Seven manuscripts agree on the date of treatise 13.

Treatise 20 was published by Favaro, "Intorno," p. 170.

the Latin names for intervals--*secunda, tercia, quarta,* and so forth--had only recently come to stand alongside the derivatives from Greek--*tonus, ditonus, diatessaron.* Antonio Favaro called his *Algorismus* an epoch-making treatise.[4] The *Scriptum super tractatu de spera Johannis de Sacrobosco* and the *Stelle fixe verificate tempore Alphonsi* are commentaries on standard astronomical texts of the day.

Prosdocimo's work made its mark. The most sophisticated of his musical treatises, the *Contrapunctus* (see no. 4 above), survives in five manuscripts, more than all but a very few of the counterpoint treatises written within seventy-five years of his. Its influence on the *Declaratio musicae disciplinae* of Ugolino was extensive and, to judge from the similarity of wording, direct. It was still being quoted in the 1530s. His *Scriptum . . . de spera* found its way into print (Venice, 1531), and his *Algorismus* was important enough to have been printed twice (Padua, 1483; Venice, 1540). Luca Pacciolli placed Prosdocimo in the distinguished company of authorities on which he drew for his *Summa de arithmetica, geometria, proportioni, et proportionalita* (Venice, 1494): "the most perspicacious Megaran philosopher Euclid and Severino Boetio, and, among our moderns, Leonardo the Pisan, Giordano, Biagio of Parma, Giovan Sacrobusco, and Prosdocimo the Paduan." Leonardo of Pisa, better known as Fibonacci, was a pioneer in the use of Hindu-Arabic numerals and the first great mathematician of Western Christendom. The *Arithmetica* of Jordanus de Nemore became the standard medieval source book for theoretical arithmetic; its author is generally regarded as the greatest medieval student of statics. Biagio Pelacani of Parma was instrumental in transmitting current scientific ideas from Paris to Italy, and was, incidentally, a sponsor of Prosdocimo's for the examination in arts. Works of Johannes de Sacrobosco became standard medieval textbooks on both arithmetic and astronomy.[5]

---

[4]Antonio Favaro, "I lettori di matematiche nella Università di Padova," in *Memorie e documenti per la storia della Università di Padova* (Padua: Garangola, 1922), pp. 32-33.

[5]Five counterpoint treatises survive in a greater number of manuscript sources than Prosdocimo's (titles follow Klaus-Jürgen Sachs, *Der Contrapunctus im 14. und 15. Jahrhundert*, Beihefte zum Archiv für Musikwissenschaft,

Was the breadth of Prosdocimo's interests unusual for a man of his day? In the Middle Ages, study of the arts was founded on the encyclopedic works of Boethius, Martianus Capella, Cassiodorus, and Isidore; medieval writers with equally comprehensive interests include Johannes Scottus Eriugena, Remi of Auxerre, Hugh of St. Victor, and Albertus Magnus. It was not unusual for medieval scholars to write on several of the arts, e.g., Gerbert of Aurillac, Engelbert of Admont, Johannes de Muris, Nicole Oresme, and Nicholas of Cusa; Nicholas may have attended Prosdocimo's lectures in astronomy. At Padua, no doctor--as

---

vol. 13 [Wiesbaden: Steiner, 1974]): *Quilibet affectans* (twelve sources), *Cum notum sit* (ten), *De diminutione contrapuncti* (ten; the three treatises just named appear together in CS, 3:59-68, as "Ars contrapuncti secundum Johannem de Muris"), *Post octavam quintam* (eight; CS, 3:116-18, as "Phillipoti Andreae De contrapuncto quaedam regulae utiles"), and *Volentibus introduci* (six, in three versions: "AC," CS, 3:12-13, as "Johannis de Garlandia Optima introductio in contrapunctum pro rudibus"; "E," CS, 3:23-27, as "Ars contrapunctus secundum Philippum de Vitriaco"; and "Pi," Sachs, *Contrapunctus*, pp. 170-73). Besides Prosdocimo's, three counterpoint treatises survive in five sources: *Nota quod unisonus de ut* (unpublished), *Quatuor principalia* 4.2 (in two versions: CS, 3:354-64, 4:278-98), Goscalcus' *Tractatus de contrapuncto* (in Oliver B. Ellsworth, "The Berkeley Manuscript [olim Phillipps 4450]: A Compendium of Fourteenth-Century Music Theory" [Ph.D. diss., University of California, Berkeley, 1969], 2 vols., 1:30-43, with English translation, 1:105-14). Tinctoris' monumental *Liber de arte contrapuncti*, for comparison, survives in but three sources.

For passages treated similarly by Prosdocimo and by Ugolino, see the Appendix.

In letters to Giovanni Spataro dated 8 October 1529 and 15 August 1533, Giovanni del Lago quoted *Contrapunctus* 5.5 and 5.3 (references to the *Contrapunctus* text are by section numbers except for references to specific variant readings, which are by page and line) in their revised versions. See F. Alberto Gallo, "Citazioni di teorici medievali nelle lettere di Giovanni del Lago," *Quadrivium* 14 (1973):176-77.

Pacciolli's list of mathematicians appears on f. 4v of the dedication of his *Summa*; information about them comes from the *Dictionary of Scientific Biography*, 16 vols. (New York: Scribner, 1970-80).

Nancy Siraisi has observed--was identified with a specific one of the arts until after the thirteenth century, and as late as the fifteenth, professors who were not *ordinarii* were expected to be able to lecture on any branch of mathematics. Like Prosdocimo, many Paduan doctors of arts were physicians as well. Of sixty members of the College of Doctors of Arts and Medicine in the late fourteenth century, Siraisi counted twenty-eight with degrees in arts and medicine as compared to thirteen in medicine alone and seven in arts alone (no information is available on the other twelve); of the five sponsors at Prosdocimo's examinations in arts and medicine, four were doctors of both.[6] Far from unique in the catholicity of his interests, Prosdocimo was a typical Paduan doctor of his day.

The Contrapunctus

"In this little work of mine," writes Prosdocimo of his *Contrapunctus*, "I do not intend to touch on all those things in this art that others have touched on; I intend only to touch on those things that seem to me necessary to it" (2.4). His "little work" is indeed a model of concision. Confining his treatment to note-against-note counterpoint for two voices, he codifies the art in six rules:

---

[6]Siraisi discusses the generalist nature of arts studies at Padua in *Arts and Sciences at Padua*, p. 68, and counts the doctors of arts and medicine on p. 30. The *Acta graduum academicorum gymnasii patavini* list Prosdocimo's sponsors, pp. 4, 42-43 (nos. 31, 155).

Italian universities, in contrast to their northern sisters, were typically organized in two colleges, one for law, one for arts and medicine. "Thus at Padua the Faculty of Arts, instead of being, as in the university centers of northern Europe, merely a preparatory stage through which aspirants to the higher faculties must pass, was itself indissolubly linked with a higher faculty, namely that of medicine" (Siraisi, *Arts and Sciences at Padua*, p. 9). The association of arts and medicine in Italy goes back to the archetypical medical school of Salerno (Hastings Rashdall, *The Universities of Europe in the Middle Ages*, 3 vols., new ed. by F. M. Powicke and A. B. Emden [Oxford: Clarendon Press, 1936], 1:83). Such writers as Isidore of Seville (*Etymologiae* 4.13.1-5) and Peter of Abano (*Conciliator*, Differentia 1) stressed the importance to the physician of studies in the arts.

1. only concords are to be used
2. a counterpoint must begin and end with a perfect concord
3. parallel perfect concords are prohibited
4. imperfect concords are not to be used continually without the occasional insertion of perfect ones
5. in fifths, octaves, and the like, mi should never be placed against fa
6. parallel imperfect concords are allowed, provided perfect ones are occasionally inserted.

These are among the most common precepts of fourteenth- and fifteenth-century music theory, but Prosdocimo's treatment of them is unique. Most authors of medieval counterpoint treatises were practical musicians trying to set down practical rules. Prosdocimo--the university man with an interest in music as one among the mathematical arts--designed to explain the principles underlying the rules. Why should counterpoint be limited to concords? Because the discords "are deeply hostile to harmony and nature, which seem to be the end of this art" (4.2). Why should parallel perfect concords be avoided? Because "one voice would sing the same as the other . . . which is not the purpose of counterpoint; its purpose is that what is sung by one voice be different from what is pronounced by the other, and that this be done through concords that are good and properly ordered" (4.4). Why should counterpoint begin and end with a perfect concord? Because the listener "should at first be moved by the harmonies that are sweeter and more amicable by nature," and "ought to be sent away with the sweetness and harmony delectable to nature, lest the listener's spirit, moved by the sweet preceding consonance, be repelled by the harshness of the final consonance from that toward which harmony is directed, enjoyment and delight" (4.3). What Prosdocimo gives us is nothing less than a primer of early fifteenth-century musical aesthetics.

Sometime after completing his *Tractatus musice speculative* in 1425--that is, during the last three years of his life--Prosdocimo revised the *Contrapunctus*. He rearranged some of the material of the original version, deleted a bit, and added a lot. Some of the revisions amplify or qualify statements from the original. Others aim at greater precision. Two of the longest insertions are criticisms of Marchetto's division of the whole tone and the chromatic signs he employed, objections that appear also in the *Tractatus musice speculative*. Perhaps what prompted Prosdocimo to revise his treatise was a desire to repudiate Marchetto's theories.[7]

---

[7]We know that the *Tractatus musice speculative* antedates the revision of the *Contrapunctus*, for Prosdocimo refers to the *Tractatus* in one of his insertions (3.9)

Prosdocimo also revised his treatises on the monochord, on plain chant, and on Italian mensural notation. The revision of the monochord treatise must have been accomplished about the same time as that of the *Contrapunctus*, for it, too, refers to the *Tractatus musice speculative*, and it likewise contains criticisms of Marchetto. (The revisions of the other two treatises cannot be dated.)

What fault did Prosdocimo find in Marchetto's division of the whole tone? In the traditional "Pythagorean" system, the whole tone had been defined by the proportion 9:8, the minor semitone by the difference between the perfect fourth and the major third (4:3÷81:64=256:243), and the major semitone by the difference between the whole tone and the minor semitone (9:8÷256:243=2187:2048). Marchetto retained the proportion 9:8 for the whole tone, but divided it into five parts and defined the two semitones simply as two-fifths and three-fifths whole tone, probably to avoid the complicated Pythagorean proportions. He also introduced intervals of one-fifth and four-fifths whole tone, which he claimed were appropriate where an imperfect consonance moves to a perfect one. He named these intervals as follows:

1/5 whole tone	diesis
2/5 whole tone	enharmonic or minor semitone
3/5 whole tone	diatonic or major semitone
4/5 whole tone	chromatic semitone or chroma

He also described a third chromatic sign that indicated division of the tone into diesis and chromatic semitone, just as the square and round b's indicate division into enharmonic (minor) and diatonic (major) semitones.

Prosdocimo objected that since the whole tone was represented by a superparticular proportion, it was impossible to divide it into five or any other number of equal parts by the means of Pythagorean mathematics; that Marchetto's usage of the term diesis contradicted that of Boethius and other theorists; that there were in fact only two semitones; and that accordingly there was no special chromatic sign to indicate division of the tone into diesis and chromatic semitone. He declared that Marchetto "purposed to write concerning things of

The revision resolves an apparent contradiction in Prosdocimo's treatment of musica ficta that has confound-

---

which he was totally ignorant" (*Contrapunctus* 3.9, insertion).

Prosdocimo's views are those of an academically oriented theorist and are literally correct. Marchetto's, on the other hand, are those of a visionary who seeks ways around the obstacles posed by traditional concepts. It is true that his system of dividing the whole tone did violate the principles of sacrosanct Pythagorean mathematics; but had those principles not been abandoned, they would have blocked the path music theory was to take over the next centuries. Marchetto's proposal set in motion a series of conjectures by theorists that led ultimately to division of the octave into twelve equal parts and made possible the development of modern harmony.

On Marchetto's division of the whole tone and its influence, see my "Marchetto's Division of the Whole Tone," *Journal of the American Musicological Society* 34 (1981):193-216; *The "Lucidarium" of Marchetto of Padua: A Critical Edition, Translation, and Commentary* (Chicago: University of Chicago Press, forthcoming); and "Fractional Divisions of the Whole Tone," *Music Theory Spectrum* 3 (1981):74-83. For details on the objections Prosdocimo raises in the *Contrapunctus*, see the annotations to the translation.

Not all of Prosdocimo's opinions of Marchetto were negative. He borrowed the discussion of the closest-approach phenomenon (*Contrapunctus* 5.6) from the *Lucidarium*. In the revision of the *Tractatus plane musice*, he wrote: "From the beginning of the *Lucidarium* to about the middle he designed to touch upon some points in the theory of music, a theory he misunderstood completely; but from roughly the middle to the end, where he turned to the practice of plain chant, he wrote uncommonly well, so that there he was beyond reproach (Multa namque scripsit in suo Lucidario que ignorabat et falsa. A principio namque Lucidarii usque circa medium tangere voluit aliqua in theorica musice, quam theoricam totaliter ignorabat. Sed a circa medium usque ad finem, ubi se transtulit ad praticam musice plane, scripsit egregie, sic quod ibi in nullo fuit reprehensione dignus [L, f. 51v])." Of the revision of the treatise on Italian mensural theory he wrote: "I have changed certain things which, as a consequence of further acquaintance with this practice, seemed to me should be changed. And these [innovations], which

ed scholars. Prosdocimo exhorts his readers to be sparing with musica ficta (5.1) and warns that "almost all composers of song very often err with respect to musica ficta, since they frequently use it where there is no necessity" (5.2). These statements are difficult to reconcile with the profusion of accidentals in Prosdocimo's single musical example (5.6):

In her penetrating essay "Musica Recta and Musica Ficta," Margaret Bent showed that we could obviate this inconsistency by assuming that Prosdocimo is advising composers "not to *write* too many accidentals but to leave them to the performers."[8] Prosdocimo must have recognized the potential for confusion here, for he takes care to resolve it in the revision: "Almost all composers of song very often err with respect to musica ficta *in notating their pieces*, since they frequently use it where there is no necessity"; this shows Bent's interpretation to be correct.

But just where is it, then, that composers err through the unnecessary use of musica ficta? Prosdocimo tells us himself, in a passage that Coussemaker garbled: "when they apply the round or soft b [i.e., the flat]

---

are somewhat at variance with the Italian notation in current use, I have taken from the *Pomerium* of Marchettus de Padua (Prosdocimus de Beldemandis, *Practice of Mensural Music in the Italian Manner*, p. 58) (Aliqua mutavi que consequenter in hac arte procedendo, michi visa sunt fore mutanda, aliquantulum discrepatia a figuratione ytalica ad presens usitata et ista extraxi ex pomerio Marcheti paduani [Sartori, *Notazione italiana del Trecento*, p. 71])." I shall discuss Prosdocimo's complex relationship to Marchetto more thoroughly in the edition of the *Tractatus musice speculative* planned for this series.

[8] *Musica Disciplina* 26 (1972):77.

in a natural signature--as on low Elami [i.e., e], because in that case they could apply the round or soft b to the signature representing square or hard ♮, high bfa♮mi [i.e., b], without any musica ficta, and that same sign would result in the piece--in its discants" (or, in the revision, "in the tenor, in the contratenor, and in the discants" [*Contrapunctus* 5.2]). For medieval writers, musica ficta was "melody brought forth outside the regular tradition of the [Guidonian] hand."[9] The regular tradition of the hand comprised the natural notes from G to e" plus the b flats in the middle and highest octaves. What Prosdocimo is telling composers is that rather than write an e-flat in the signature--an operation that requires musica ficta--they could simply supply a b-flat in the signature and leave it to performers to supply a flat for the e in accord with *Contrapunctus* 5.6:

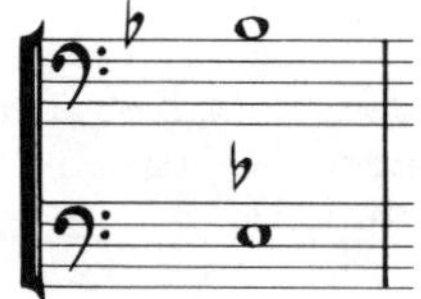

That is precisely what happens in a *Patrem* by Prosdocimo's Paduan contemporary Ciconia:[10]

---

[9]"Ficta musica est cantus praeter regularem manus traditionem aeditus" (Johannis Tinctoris, *Dictionary of Musical Terms*, ed. Carl Parrish [Glencoe: Free Press, 1963], pp. 32-33, as corrected by Edward E. Lowinsky, "Renaissance Writings on Music Theory [1964]," *Renaissance News* 18 [1965]:361-62).

[10]Ciconia, No. 28, mm. 133-36. Suzanne Clercx, *Johannes Ciconia: Un musicien liégois et son temps (vers 1335-1411)*, 2 vols., Académie Royale de Belgique, Classe des Beaux-Arts, Mémoires, no. 10 (Brussels: Palais des Académies, 1960), 2:138. Similar situations appear in mm. 76-79, 90, 102, 105-7, and 128. A flat is applied directly to e in m. 163, where no b sounds in another part. The piece appears in I-Bc Q 15.

Scholars who favor caution in the introduction of editorial accidentals sometimes enlist Prosdocimo in their support. But his position could not be further from theirs. First, there is the audacity of his musical example with its many chromatic signs. Second, there is his justification of the tenor c#' that results in an augmented-fourth leap: the c' must be sharped to bring the sixth that contains it closer to the sixth that follows (*Contrapunctus* 5.6). Medieval theorists allowed the chromatic alteration of an imperfect consonance progressing immediately to a perfect one: the effect is more perfect, as Prosdocimo notes in the original version of his treatise, "the closer the imperfect consonance approaches the perfect one it intends to reach." In the revision, Prosdocimo rewords this statement to allow for progressions to any consonance, perfect or imperfect: the effect is more perfect "the closer the imperfect consonance approaches *the other consonance* it intends immediately to reach." The scholars who ought to take succor from Prosdocimo's words are those who are boldest in the application of editorial accidentals.

Prosdocimo's Place

Prosdocimo stands at the junction of two eras. He is a man of the Middle Ages. His is the age of the Pythagorean tuning system (to which he adhered, as we know from his treatises on proportions and the monochord); of harmony based on empty fifths and octaves; of isorhythm; of the double-leading-tone cadence. He is a champion of the Italian system of mensural notation at a time when it is already moribund. But in one respect Prosdocimo is thoroughly a man of the Renaissance, and he shows this modernity most clearly at the end of his revision of the *Contrapunctus*, where he explains the application of musica ficta. "I advise you to be circumspect in applying these signs," he writes, "because they should be applied where they sound more agreeable. If they sound better in the tenor, they should be applied in the tenor; if they sound better in the discant, they should be applied in the discant. . . . *Knowing where the signs sound better I leave to your ear.*" Marchetto of Padua articulated the typically medieval predilection for the intellect over the senses in aesthetic matters: "The judgment of music does not lie in sound alone, for the sense of hearing can be deceived, like the other bodily senses. The sense of sight is deceived when a straight stick is placed in water: it is perceived by the eyes as crooked. And the sense of hearing is very often deceived when it is charmed by a sound devoid of any ratio or proportion."[11] Prosdocimo's words--"knowing where the signs sound better I leave to your ear"--advocate the senses as the basis for aesthetic judgment. They stand the medieval attitude on its head, and articulate, for the first time in the history of music theory, one principle of the musical aesthetic of the Renaissance.

The Manuscripts

The original version of Prosdocimo's *Contrapunctus* survives in four manuscripts:[12]

B

Bologna, Civico Museo Bibliografico Musicale (I-Bc)
A.56 (Martini, 4)

Paper; 268 pages, ca. 32.5x23.0 cm
Sabbioncello (near Ferrara), 1437

The manuscript consists of thirteen quinios and a final binio (probably originally another quinio from

---

[11]Marchetto, *Lucidarium* 4.2-3: "Non est iudicium musice solum in sono, quia sensus auditus potest falli, ut et ceteri sensus corporis; nam fallitur sensus visus si rectum lignum in aqua ponatur, quia conspicitur oculis tortuosum. Fallitur etiam sensus auditus sepius cum delectatur in sono ab omni ratione et proportione remoto" (Herlinger ed.).

[12]The descriptions incorporate information from Gallo, "Trattati di Prosdocimo," passim.

which the middle sheets were lost, since Prosdocimo's *Tractatus musice speculative* breaks off abruptly just at the middle of the gathering) bound in boards (ca. 33.5x23.0 cm) with a leather spine. There are four paper flyleaves at the front, three at the rear.

Two columns of 24x7 cm are marked off on each page, separated by a space of 1.5 cm with margins of 2.5 cm at the top, 6 cm at the bottom, 4.5 cm at the outside edge, and 3 cm at the inside edge (measurements are approximate, as there is ca. 0.5 cm variation in size from one page to another). The text was written by a single hand, with forty-three to fifty lines per column. According to a colophon from one of the sheets now missing from the last gathering, the manuscript was copied by Antonius de Obizis of Lucca and completed at Sabbioncello (district of Ferrara) on 21 August 1437.[13] The text is in light brown ink with ornate initials--many decorated with fine vertical lines--in red and blue. The pages were numbered 1-268 in their upper outside corners after the loss of the center sheets of the last gathering.

The manuscript contains only treatises of Prosdocimo:

1. *Expositiones tractatus pratice cantus mensurabilis magistri Johannis de Muris* (pp. 1-72)
2. *De parallelogramo* (p. 73)
3. *Tractatus pratice cantus mensurabilis* (pp. 74-91 [p. 92 blank])
4. *Brevis summula proportionum quantum ad musicam pertinet* (pp. 93-95 [p. 96 blank])
5. *Contrapunctus* (pp. 97-100)
6. *Tractatus pratice cantus mensurabilis ad modum Ytalicorum* (pp. 101-13) [p. 114 blank])
7. *Tractatus plane musice* (pp. 115-33 [p. 134 blank])
8. *Brevis tractatulus de electionibus secundum situm lune in suis 28 mansionibus* (pp. 135-37 [p. 138 blank])

---

[13]The colophon is recorded by Giacomo Filippo Tomasin, *Bibliothecae patavinae manuscriptae publicae et privatae quibus diversi scriptores hactenus incogniti recensentur ac illustrantur* (Udine, 1639), p. 128, and quoted by Gallo, "Trattati di Prosdocimo," p. 66: "Et ego Antonius quondam Roberti de Obizis de Luca totum hunc librum scripsi, atque complevi Sablonzelli districtus Ferrariensis die Mercurii xxi Augusti 1437."

9. *Parvus tractatulus de modo monacordum dividendi* (pp. 139-45 [p. 146 blank])
10. *Scriptum super tractatu de spera Johannis de Sacrobosco Anglici* (pp. 147-229)
11. *Canon in quo docetur modus componendi et operandi tabulam quandam* (pp. 230-33)
12. *Algorismus de integris sive pratica arismetrice de integris* (pp. 234-47)
13. *De progressionibus* (p. 247)
14. *Tractatus musice speculative*, incomplete at the end (pp. 248-64 [pp. 265-68 blank]).

Thus the manuscript transmits all Prosdocimo's musical treatises in chronological order, the most important of his treatises on arithmetic and astronomy, and his sole surviving work on geometry.

The text of the *Contrapunctus* in B is excellent, free of errors except for a very few minor ones, e.g., *infimum* for *infinitum* (see p. 36.9).

C

Cremona, Biblioteca Governativa (I-CR) 252[14]

Parchment; 41 folios, ca. 20.0x14.5 cm
Italy; fifteenth century

The manuscript consists of four quinios preceded by a single leaf, with the leaves numbered 1-41 in the lower left corners of their recto sides. An earlier numbering system used the letters c-f to represent the four complete gatherings presently in the manuscript, numbering the five bifolia of each gathering 1-5 in the lower right corners of the recto sides of their front halves. The single leaf at the front of the manuscript is numbered 6. The first and last treatises of the manuscript are incomplete. Hence we can infer that there were originally two additional gatherings at the front of the manuscript (at least one of which consisted of six or more bifolia; the single sheet surviving was the front half of the sixth bifolium of one of these) and one or more additional gatherings at the end. The binding (21.0x15.0 cm) is pasteboard.

A writing area of 14.5x9 cm is marked off on each leaf, leaving margins of 2 cm at the top, 3.5 cm at the bottom, 4 cm at the outside edge, and 1.5 cm at the inside

---

[14]Not "238" as Gallo has it, "Trattati di Prosdocimo," p. 69.

edge. The text was written by a single hand, with thirty lines of text per page. Starting on f. 24, the writing seems more hurried and less regular. The main text is in light brown ink, with initials--decorated with fine vertical lines--in red and blue. The vertical lines, plus the uncrossed tironian *et* sign (⁊) and the abbreviation ꝗ for *qui*, attest to the Italian provenance of the manuscript. The scribe's spelling is characterized by the use of double *l* between vowels (e.g., *regulla, volluerunt, tallis*) and the frequent use of *sc* for *s* (e.g., *muscica, uscitantur*).

The manuscript as it stands contains only works of Prosdocimo:

1. *Tractatus plane musice*, incomplete (ff. 1rv [internal fragment], 2r-9r [end], f. 9v blank)
2. *Contrapunctus* (ff. 10r-15v)
3. *Tractatus pratice cantus mensurabilis*, incomplete at the end (ff. 16r-41v).

These are Prosdocimo's treatises on the three most fundamental topics of music: plain chant, counterpoint, and mensuration.

The text of the *Contrapunctus* is quite good, but is marred by small errors, e.g., *dissonantias* om. p. 38.7; *discordantes* om. p. 48.2-3; *mi* om. p. 76.7; *unius* for *minus*, p. 86.12; and two substantial omissions, p. 50.12-16 and p. 86.5-9, brought about by *saut du même au même*. Some variants may represent intentional stylistic revisions, e.g., *est* for *reperitur quelibet*, p. 44.1; *a* for *semper de*, p. 52.18; *fieret* for *foret*, p. 68.1.

E

Einsiedeln, Benediktinerkloster (CH-E) 689[15]

Parchment; 96 folios, ca. 14.0-14.5x10.5-11.0 cm
Italy; early fifteenth century

The manuscript consists of gatherings of two, three, and four double sheets of parchment, somewhat irregu-

---

[15]Not "684" as Favaro has it, "Intorno," pp. 236-37; or "638" as in *The Theory of Music from the Carolingian era up to 1400, Volume 1*, ed. Joseph Smits van Waesberghe, Répertoire international des sources musicales, B III[1] (Munich-Duisburg: Henle, 1961), p. 75; or "Cod. 385" as in Giuseppe Vecchi, "Su la composizione del *Pomerium* di

lar in size and varying in color from cream through yellow to light brown. Of the ninety-six folios the first ten are unnumbered; the others are numbered I-LVI and LXXV-CIIII in red and blue ink in the upper middle of the recto sides. Missing are eighteen folios in the middle of the manuscript and at least twelve folios at the end. A writing area of 8.9x6.7 cm is marked off on each sheet, with margins of approximately 1.8 cm at the top, 3.6 cm at the bottom, 2.5 cm at the outer edge, and 1.4 cm at the inner edge. Generally there are twenty-eight lines of text per page, sometimes a few more or less. On ff. 51-56 and 75-80 the writing area tends to be somewhat longer and wider, but with no more lines of text per page; in item 8 the writing is quite irregular. Construction and contents are as follows:

Folios/ Gathering	Contents
[a-d]	1. Table of contents (ff. [a]r-[g]r [ff. (g)v-(j)v blank])
[e-j]	
1-8	2. Marchetto, *Lucidarium* (Herlinger ed.) (ff. 1r-44r [f. 44v blank])
9-12	
13-16	
17-24	
25-32	
33-40	
41-44	
45-50	3. Treatise on counterpoint, *Volentibus introduci*, version E (CS, 3:12-13, as "Johannis de Garlandia Optima introductio in contrapunctum pro rudibus") (f. 45v)
	4. Treatise on counterpoint, *Post octavam quintam* (CS, 3:116-18, as "Phillipoti Andreae De contrapuncto quaedam regulae utiles") (f. 45v)
	5. Treatise on counterpoint, *Volentibus introduci*, version AC (CS, 3:23-27, as "Ars contrapunctus secundum Philippum de Vitriaco") (ff. 46r-50r [f. 50v blank])
51-56	6. Prosdocimo, *Contrapunctus* (ff. 51r-55r [f. 55v-56v blank])
57-74	missing (the table of contents lists a treatise identical in content to Prosdocimo's *Tractatus pratice cantus mensurabilis*)

Marchetto da Padova e la *Brevis compilatio*," *Quadrivium* 1 (1956):154.

75-82	7. Prosdocimo, *Parvus tractatulus de modo monacordum dividendi* (ff. 75r-80v)
	8. Treatise on the monochord, "Monacordum tuum sic dividas. Primo totum spacium interceptum inter primum C et punctum scabelli in novem partes equales dividas. . . ." (unedited) (ff. 81r-82v)
83-90	9. Johannes de Muris, *Libellus cantus mensurabilis* (CS, 3:46-58) (ff. 83r-90v)
91-98 99-104	10. Johannes de Muris, *Musica speculativa*, version B (*Scriptores ecclesiastici de musica sacra potissimum*, 3 vols., ed. Martin Gerbert [St. Blaise, 1784; reprint ed., Milan: Bollettino Bibliografico Musicale, 1931], 3:256-83) (ff. 91r-104v)
105-116+	missing (the table of contents lists a *Tractatus proportionum secundum Antonium Monachum ac Paduanum*[16]).

Five scribes worked on the manuscript:

1. Items 1 and 2. A fine, slightly rounded gothic book hand. The d is uncial, and the straight and round forms of the r are correctly used for the most part. Juncture is sometimes real, but at other times strokes that appear to be joined merely overlap.
2. Items 3 and 4. A less careful and less correctly written (e.g., the round r is frequently used after letters that are not round), tiny gothic book hand. The d is uncial.
3. Items 5, 6, and 7. A hand similar to that of scribe 2, but with an upright d except in the headlines--which may be in a different hand. The round r is used exclusively.
4. Item 8. This is a large, crude hand. The d is uncial, the r round. Juncture is not used.

---

[16]Perhaps the author of this treatise is the Antonius de Lydo, "clericus Paduanus," who was enrolled at Paris in 1349 (*Chartularium Universitatis Parisiensis*, 4 vols., ed. Henri Denifle [Paris: Delalain, 1891], 2:634). According to Bernardino Scardeone (*De antiquitate urbis patavii et claris civibus patavinis libri tres* [Basle, 1560], p. 262), Antonius studied philosophy and all the arts, chiefly music, and his epitaph (1385) described him as "artist in music, Parisian doctor." See Siraisi, *Arts and Sciences at Padua*, p. 107.

5. Items 9 and 10. A small, neat gothic book hand. The d is uncial; straight and round forms of the r are used, not always correctly. Real juncture is rare; more often, strokes merely overlap.

Headlines are red; initials are alternately red with blue decoration and blue with red decoration (the decoration is omitted in items 6 and 7). Initials are missing entirely in item 8.

Since the manuscript includes Prosdocimo's treatise on the monochord, it cannot have been copied before 1413. The very fine gothic characteristics of scribe 1 make a date very far into the fifteenth century unlikely.

This is a carefully prepared manuscript, designed to encompass the entire field of music theory--plain chant (item 2), counterpoint (3, 4, 5, 6), mensuration (9 and the treatise on the missing folios 57-74), the monochord (7), and proportions (the missing treatise at the end of the manuscript). Item 8 must be a later addition, as it is not listed in the table of contents and was copied by a hand inconsistent with the rest of the manuscript.

The text of Prosdocimo's *Contrapunctus* is quite good but idiosyncratic. The five sections of the treatise are provided with headlines. As noted above, these headlines may be in a different hand from the main text; the manner in which they are fitted between lines and in the margins suggests that they were an afterthought. The scribe has designated the diminished ("minor") fifth and octave as having no "firm proportion" (see pp. 44.15 and 46.11)--meaning probably that their proportions are not obtained by simple divisions of the monochord--and regularly refers to the minor and major semitones as "enharmonic" and "diatonic," following Marchetto's usage.

V

Vatican City, Biblioteca Apostolica Vaticana (I-Rvat)
Vaticanus latinus 5321

Paper; 25 folios, ca. 29-29.5x20-20.5 cm
Italy; fifteenth century

The manuscript consists of a single sheet (f. 1), two quinios (2-11, 12-21), and a four-sheet gathering of uncertain construction (22-25). The sheets are numbered 1-25 in pencil in the upper right corners of their recto sides (in an earlier system, sheets 2-25 had been numbered 1-24 in ink in the upper right corners). The manuscript is bound in leather-covered boards, ca. 30x21.5 cm.

Folios 2-13 and 17-25 are marked off in double columns, ca. 19-19.5x5.6 cm, separated by 2.1 cm, with margins of 3.5-4 cm at the top, 6-6.5 cm at the bottom, 4-5 cm at the outside edge, and 2-3 cm at the inside edge; folios 14-16, which contain large diagrams, are marked in single columns of ca. 19x13 cm, with margins of ca. 4 cm at the top, ca. 6 cm at the bottom, ca. 5 cm at the outside edge, and ca. 2.5 cm at the inside edge. The first sheet is copied in a humanistic hand, the rest in a gothic book hand with ornate initials in red and blue.

Contents are as follows:

1. Treatise on notes, hexachords, and modes, "Quot sunt iuncture manus? . . ." (unedited) (f. 1r [f. 1v blank])
2. Johannes de Muris, *Libellus cantus mensurabilis* (ff. 2r-6r)
3. Egidius de Murino, *Tractatus cantus mensurabilis* (CS, 3:118-28, as "Philippi de Caserta Tractatus de diversis figuris" and "Magistri Aegidii de Murino Tractatus cantus mensurabilis") (ff. 6r-9v)
4. Prosdocimo, *Contrapunctus* (ff. 9v-11v)
5. Johannes de Muris, *Musica speculativa*, version B, fragment (ff. 12r-20r)
6. Prosdocimo, *Canon in quo docetur modus componendi et operandi tabulam quandam* (ff. 20r-22r [f. 22v blank])
7. Treatise on counterpoint, *Volentibus introduci*, version AC (ff. 23r-25v)
8. Treatise on counterpoint, *Quilibet affectans* (f. 25v).

The text of the *Contrapunctus* is poor. Three short omissions result from *saut du même au même* (see pp. 36.3-4, 52.5-6, and 74.2-3). Other variants simply produce nonsense, e.g., *sunt* for *Perfecte sunt*, p. 42.2; *actiones* for *auctores*, p. 46.7; *duorum* for *durum*, p. 74.10.

The revision of the *Contrapunctus* survives in a single source:

L

Lucca, Biblioteca Governativa (I-Lg) 359

Paper; 98 folios, ca. 29.5x21.5 cm
Italy; between 1425 and 1477

The manuscript consists of nine quinios numbered (in light brown ink, in the upper right corners of the recto sides) 2-91 plus eight sheets in a gathering of uncertain construction numbered 92, 93, 106-10, 115.[17] It is contained in a modern brown leather binding, 30x22.5 cm.

The pages are marked off in double columns of 17.3x5.7 cm separated by ca. 1.1 cm, with margins of ca. 4.5 cm at the top, 7.5-8 cm at the bottom, 5.5-6 cm at the outside edge, and 2.5-3 cm at the inside edge. The text was copied in light to medium brown ink in a very beautiful gothic book hand, with forty lines of text per column. The treatises begin with elaborate initials in red, blue, green, and gold; otherwise, initials are in red and brown ink.

Contents of the manuscript are as follows:

1. Prosdocimo, *Tractatus pratice cantus mensurabilis* (ff. 2r-27v)
2. Prosdocimo, *Contrapunctus* (ff. 28r-33v)
3. Prosdocimo, *Tractatus pratice cantus mensurabilis ad modum Ytalicorum* (ff. 34r-48r [f. 48v blank])
4. Prosdocimo, *Tractatus plane musice* (ff. 49r-71r [f. 71v blank])
5. Prosdocimo, *Parvus tractatulus de modo monacordum dividendi* (ff. 72r-78r [f. 78v blank])
6. Prosdocimo, *Tractatus musice speculative* (ff. 79r-93r [f. 93v blank])
7. *Ars musice plane optima et perfecta*, incomplete (unedited) (ff. 106r-110v, 115r [115v blank])

The manuscript contains Prosdocimo's *Tractatus musice speculative* of 1425. According to a note on f. 98r, it was donated to the Paduan monastery of San Giovanni in Verdara by Pietro Montagnana, who died in 1477. The manuscript must have been copied between those dates.

The Edition

Coussemaker knew four of the Prosdocimo manuscripts, B, E, L (which he calls a Paduan source), and V. According to his preface, he utilized B for the *Tractatus pratice cantus mensurabilis*, the *Brevis summula proportionum*, and the *Tractatus pratice cantus mensurabilis ad modum Ytalicorum*; both B and E for the *Parvus tractatulus de modo monacordum dividendi*. He seems to have relied on B and E for the *Contrapunctus* also; in the entire treatise

---

[17]Gallo reads the last folio number as 119, "Trattati di Prosdocimo," p. 79.

there are only two instances where his text agrees with readings peculiar to L or V (*tracta* for *tacta* in agreement with V [see p. 32.14]; *que armonia* for *que* in agreement with L [see p. 58.8]), and these may be accidental. There is, in fact, no other evidence that he consulted L or V. His partiality toward E is patent. He retained its unique headlines, followed its word order where that diverged from B's, and even twice transcribed E's erroneous reading of *precessoribus* for *predecessoribus* (see pp. 26.6 and 34.8). In only two instances did he choose readings from B over those of E: B's *sed* over E's *sed et* (p. 26.7), B's *super* over E's *supra* (p. 32.6). He also retained E's idiosyncratic use of Marchetto's terms *semitonium enarmonicum* and *dyatonicum* for the minor and major semitones. In the light of Prosdocimo's criticism of Marchetto's terminology, it is ironic that it was this version of the *Contrapunctus* that Coussemaker chose to present to the world.

The present edition is based on all five manuscript versions of the *Contrapunctus*. The text is presented at the top of each verso page, with variant readings from the five manuscripts at the bottom.[18] Medieval orthography is retained, but with i/j, u/v, c/t before i plus vowel, double consonants, assimilation, and the like normalized. Prosdocimo's revisions, transmitted in L, are presented between the main text and variants.[19] English translations of the main text and Prosdocimo's revisions appear on facing recto pages. Comments appear at the bottom of the rectos. These serve to explain the text, trace quotations, and link Prosdocimo's ideas with those of other theorists, primarily contrapuntal theorists of the fourteenth and fifteenth centuries.

---

[18] Variants are reported by line. Generally a *lemma* from the text is given, followed by the sigla of the sources that support it, the variant, and the siglum of its source. Where the *lemma* is obvious it is omitted. Subsequent variants in the same line are separated by a single vertical line, subsequent lines by a double vertical line.

[19] It is sometimes impossible to know whether a particular variant in L is inadvertent or conscious on the part of Prosdocimo (or of a scribe). Accordingly, only those that significantly alter the meaning are reported between main text and variants; the others are relegated to the variants.

CONSPECTUS CODICUM ET NOTARUM

Manuscripts

B	Bononiensis A.56 (1437), I-Bc
L	Lucensis 359 (between 1425 and 1477), I-Lg
E	Einsidlensis 689 (early 15th century), CH-E
C	Cremonensis 252 (15th century), I-CR
V	Vaticanus 5321 (15th century), I-Rvat

Earlier Edition

CS *Scriptorum de musica medii aevi nova series a Gerbertina altera*, 4 vols., ed. Edmond de Coussemaker (Paris: Durand, 1864-1876), 3:193-99

Notes

alt.	altered
ante	before
bis	twice
cantus inferior	lower melody
del.	deleted
et	and
ex	from
fort.	perhaps
in marg.	in margin
inter	between
legi non potest	cannot be read
m. sec.	in a second hand
om.	omitted
post	after
pr.	first
sec.	second
sine	without
sup. lin.	above the line
tit.	title
transcriptio exempli in semibrevibus	transcription of the example in semibreves
ut	like
verb. illeg.	illegible word

Dots under letters indicate uncertain transcription.
Double square brackets indicate deletions of more than a single word by the scribe.

<CONTRAPUNCTUS>

1

1. Scribit Aristotiles secundo Elenchorum, capitulo ultimo, facile fore inventis addere, et ex hoc || dignissimum esse de inventis infinitas inventoribus habere grates, quod etiam assero, qua de re in hoc meo opusculo, in quo intendo de contrapuncto determinare, non intendo in aliquo predecessoribus nostris, qui circa hanc artem laboraverunt, obviare, sed eadem tangere que et ipse || tetigerunt, licet diversimode, aliqua tamen per modernos usitata reprobando. CS CS

---

1 *Tit.*: Tractatus primus de contrapunctu, Capitulum primum, Prologus *fort. m. sec.* E Incipit Contrapunctus Magistri Prosdocimi de Beldemandis patavi V || 2 et *om.* V || 6 precessoribus E deprecessoribus V || 7 sed]sed et E | contingerunt V || 8 tamen *om.* C | reprobando]et obprobando V ||

COUNTERPOINT

1

1. Aristotle writes in the Second Book of the *Refutations*, last chapter, that it will be easy to add to what has been discovered, and that it is therefore most proper to give infinite thanks to the discoverers of that which has been discovered.[1] This I affirm. Hence in this little work of mine, in which I intend to treat of counterpoint, I do not intend in any way to oppose our predecessors who labored at this art, but to touch on that on which they touched, though in a different manner, rejecting some things customary among modern writers.

---

[1]Aristotle *De sophisticis elenchis* 34 (183b25-26). The normal spelling of the philosopher's name was "Aristotiles" during the Middle Ages, in contrast to the classical "Aristoteles"; see Richard C. Dales, review of Robert Grosseteste, *Commentarius in posteriorum analyticorum libros*, ed. Pietro Rossi, in *Speculum* 57 (1982):616.

2

1. Quia igitur cantum contra cantum sumere duobus modis inveniri potest, scilicet quando plures note contra unicam solam notam sumuntur et supra vel infra ipsam scribi vel cantari habent, et quando unica sola nota contra aliam unicam solam sumitur et supra vel infra ipsam scribi vel cantari habet, est sciendum quod contrapunctus potest sumi dupliciter, scilicet comuniter sive large et proprie sive stricte. Contrapunctus largo modo sive comuniter sumptus est plurium notarum contra aliquam unicam solam notam in aliquo cantu positio, et de tali non intendo hic determinare, nec talis vere contrapunctus nominari habet; contrapunctus vero proprie sive stricte sumptus est unius solius note contra aliquam aliam unicam solam notam in aliquo cantu positio, et de tali hic bene intendo determinare, cum hic vere contrapunctus nominari habeat, eo quod in ipso est vera contrapositio, quia scilicet

---

1 *Tit.*: Capitulum primum *fort. m. sec.* E | igitur]igitur *vel* ergo V | cantum contra cantum] c̄anatum (=?) contra c̄anatum (=?) V || 1-2 sumere . . . potest]duobus modis sumere potest C || 2 inveniri *ex* invenitur *alt.* E | potest]possunt V | inveniri potest]invenitur L | scilicet]uno scilicet modo L | note]notes C || 3 ipsam *om.* C || 4 et]et alio modo L || 5 solam]solam notam L | *post* infra sc *del.* C | scribi vel *in marg.* E || 7-8 et proprie sive . . . largo modo sive *om.* C || 8 *post* Contrapunctus vero *del.* B | largo modo *om.* V || 10 tali]tali contrapuncto L || 11 hic *sup. lin.* B | vere]nature B || 11-12 nominari habet]nominatur E || 12 proprie sive *om.* C || 13 aliam *om.* V || 14 tali hic bene intendo]tali contrapuncto bene intendo hic L || 15 *post* determinare [[nec talis vere contrapunctus]] *del.* L || 16 *post* contrapositio [[vere est contrapositio]] *del.* E ||

1. Because it can be found that the phrase "melody against melody" is construed in two ways--when many notes are employed against a single note and are to be written or sung above or below it, and when a single note is employed against another single note and is to be written or sung above or below it--it must be known that counterpoint can also be construed in two ways, in the ordinary or loose sense and in the proper or strict sense. Counterpoint construed in the ordinary or loose sense is the placement of many notes against one single note in a melody, and this sort I do not intend to treat here; nor is this sort truly to be called counterpoint. Counterpoint construed in the proper or strict sense is the placement of one single note against some other single note in a melody, and this sort I do intend to treat here, since this sort is truly to be called counterpoint, because in it there is a true counterplacement, the counterplacement

contrapositio note contra notam, que contrapositio vere est interpretatio istius termini contrapunctus, cum contrapunctus dicatur quasi contrapositio note scilicet contra notam, quando scilicet nota supra vel infra notam scribi vel cantari habet, et est huiusmodi contrapunctus proprie sumptus alterius comuniter sumpti fundamentum, eo quod habita noticia huius, statim haberi potest noticia alterius, saltim apud usitatos circa cantum fractibilem.

1-4 que contrapositio . . . contra notam *om.* L || 2 termini *legi non potest* V || 2-3 cum contrapunctus *om.* B || 4 notam (*sec.*)]aliam notam L || 5 huiusmodi]huius V || 5-6 proprie sumptus (sumptus *in marg.*) contrapunctus E || 6 alterius]alterius contrapuncti L | comuniter]comunius V | fundamentum *in marg.* E || 7 huius]contrapuncti proprie sumpti L | *post* huius h *del.* E | alterius]contrapuncti comuniter sumpti L || 8 saltim *legi non potest* V ||

of note against note. This counterplacement is the true meaning of the term counterpoint, since counterpoint is defined as the counterplacement of note against note--one note to be written or sung above or below the other note.[1] Counterpoint construed in the proper sense is the foundation of the other, construed in the ordinary sense, because with understanding of the one, one can straightway have understanding of the other, of the practice of florid song.[2]

---

[1]For a history of the term *contrapunctus*, see Klaus-Jürgen Sachs, *Der Contrapunctus im 14. und 15. Jahrhundert*, Beihefte zum Archiv für Musikwissenschaft, vol. 13 (Wiesbaden: Steiner, 1974), pp. 24-56.

Ugolino of Orvieto borrowed Prosdocimo's distinction between *contrapunctus stricte seu proprie sumptus* (or *contrapunctus simplex*) and *contrapunctus large sumptus*; see his *Declaratio* 2.2.2, 4-6 (*Ugolini Urbevetani declaratio musicae disciplinae*, 3 vols., ed. Albert Seay, Corpus scriptorum de musica, no. 7 [Rome: American Institute of Musicology, 1959-1962], 2:4). Other theorists found other terms to distinguish between note-against-note and florid counterpoint, just as Prosdocimo had: *simplex/copulatus* (*Quatuor principalia* 4.2.11 [*Scriptorum de musica medii aevi nova series a Gerbertina altera* (henceforward: CS), 4 vols., ed. Edmond de Coussemaker (Paris: Durand, 1864-1876), 4:278a]); *contrapunctus simplex/diminutus* (Tinctoris, *Liber de arte contrapuncti* 2.19.2-8 [*Johannis Tinctoris opera theoretica*, 2 vols., ed. Albert Seay, Corpus scriptorum de musica, no. 22 (N.p.: American Institute of Musicology, 1975), 2:105-7]); *cantus commixtus/cantus figuratus* (Burzio, *Florum libellus* 2.Praef.5-6 [*Nicolai Burtii Parmensis florum libellus*, ed. Giuseppe Massera, Historiae musicae cultores, Biblioteca, no. 28 (Florence: Olschki, 1975), p. 115]).

[2]On note-against-note counterpoint as the basis of florid counterpoint, cf. *Cum notum sit* (CS, 3:60b); Goscalcus, *Tractatus de contrapuncto* (Oliver B. Ellsworth, "The Berkeley Manuscript [olim Phillipps 4450]: A Compendium of Fourteenth-Century Music Theory" [Ph.D. diss., University of California, Berkeley, 1969], 2 vols., 1:35); Legrense, *Ritus canendi vetustissimus et novus* 2.3 (CS, 4:383b-384a); Burzio, *Florum libellus* Praef. 6 (Massera ed., p. 115).

2. Item sciendum quod huiusmodi contrapunctus, scilicet proprius, est duplex, scilicet vocalis et scriptus: vocalis qui profertur et scriptus qui scribitur, de quibus ambobus intelligenda sunt omnia que de contrapuncto inferius dicentur, ex || quo sequitur contrapunctum comuniter acceptum, CS 19 qui ex proprio accepto sequitur et super ipso fundatur, etiam esse duplicem, scilicet vocalem et scriptum, et vocalem esse illum qui profertur et scriptum qui scribitur.

3. Item sciendum quod hec ars contrapuncti artem pratice cantus plani presupponit, absque qua nichil huiusmodi scientie haberi poterit.

4. Item sciendum, ne admiratio aliqua tibi insurgat, quod in hoc meo tractatulo non intendo omnia tangere que ab aliis in hac arte tacta sunt, sed solum illa tangere intendo que huic arti michi neccessaria videbuntur.

1-5 *Huc pertinet emendatio quae in L invenitur:* Preterea uterque istorum contrapunctorum est duplex, vocalis scilicet et scriptus: vocalis qui profertur et scriptus qui scribitur, et tam de vocali quam de scripto contrapuncto proprie sumpto intelligenda sunt omnia que de contrapuncto inferius dicentur, . . . 9-11 *Huc pertinet emendatio quae in L post paragraphum 1 invenitur:* Uterque tamen istorum contrapunctorum artem pratice cantus plani presupponit, absque qua nichil huius artis contrapuncti haberi potest [*ms.:* post]. 12-13 *Huc pertinet emendatio quae in L invenitur:* Ne tamen admiratio aliqua tibi insurgat, volo te scire quod in hoc meo tractatulo . . .

---

2 *ante* est [[artem pratice cantus]] *del.* L | et scriptus: vocalis *in marg.* B || 3 et *om.* C || 4 omnia]per omnia V || 5-8 ex quo . . . qui scribitur *om.* L || 6 supra E || 7 et (*sec.*) *legi non potest* V || 8 qui scribitur *legi non potest* V || 10 abque E || 10-11 scientie huiusmodi C || 14 in hac arte *om.* V in arte hac L | tacta]tracta V || 14-15 intendo tangere illa C || 15 michi *om.* V ||

2. It must be known, too, that counterpoint taken in the proper sense is twofold, vocal and written: vocal, that which is uttered, and written, that which is notated. Everything that will be said of counterpoint below is to be understood to pertain to both. From this, it follows that counterpoint taken in the ordinary sense--which follows from that taken in the proper sense and is founded upon it--is also twofold, vocal and written: vocal, that which is uttered, and written, that which is notated.

3. It must be known, too, that the art of counterpoint presupposes the art of plain chant practice, without which nothing of this science will be understood.[3]

4. It must be known, too, lest your wonder be aroused, that in this little work of mine I do not intend to touch on all those things in this art that others have touched on; I intend only to touch on those things that seem to me necessary to it.

1-5: Moreover, either of these two sorts of counterpoint is twofold, vocal and written: vocal, that which is uttered, and written, that which is notated. Everything that will be said of counterpoint below is to be understood to pertain as much to vocal as to written counterpoint, construed in the proper sense. 9-11: Either of these two sorts of counterpoint presupposes the art of plain chant practice, without which nothing of the art of counterpoint can be understood. 12-13: Lest your wonder be aroused, I want you to know that in this little work of mine . . .

---

[3]On plain chant as the basis of counterpoint, cf. Franco, *Ars cantus mensurabilis*, Prol. 1 (*Franconis de Colonia ars cantus mensurabilis*, ed. Gilbert Reaney and André Gilles, Corpus scriptorum de musica, no. 18 [N.p.: American Institute of Musicology, 1974], p. 23); *Cum notum sit* (CS, 3:60a); Ugolino, *Declaratio* 2.4.2 (Seay ed., 2:8); Legrense, *Ritus canendi vetustissimus et novus* 2.3 (CS, 4:383b-384a). Sachs finds further instances in unpublished treatises; see his *Contrapunctus*, p. 53.

3

1. Hiis ergo sic declaratis, ad declarationem combinationum vocum accedamus, unde dico quod vocum combinatio est duarum vocum consonantiam vel dissonantiam auribus reddentium insimul agregatio, et intelligo per voces, voces musicales, que sunt sex, scilicet ut, re, mi, fa, sol, la.

2. Ulterius dico quod combinationes vocum in hac arte nominari solite ab omnibus nostris predecessoribus quamplures esse recitantur, scilicet unisonus, secunda, tercia, quarta, quinta, sexta, septima, et octava, que tantum valet quantum unisonus, quoniam omnis cantus inceptus in unisono inchoari potest in octava, et e contra; item una nona, que tantum valet quantum una secunda propter causam dictam; et una decima, que propter causam dictam

---

7-9 *Huc pertinet emendatio quae in L invenitur:* . . . combinationes vocum in hac arte nominari solite ab omnibus nostris predecessoribus quamplures esse recitantur atque hiis nominibus modernis nominantur, . . .

---

1 *Tit.*: Tractatus secundus, De declaratione combinationum, Capitulum primum *fort. m. sec.* E | ergo]itaque L | declarationem]declarandum vel declarationem V || 2-4 vocum combinatio . . . agregatio]combinatio vocum est agregatio duarum vocum consonantiam vel dissonantiam auribus reddentium L || 4 intelligo]intelligo hic L || 5 musicales *ex* mutabiles *alt.* E | *post* sunt se *del.* V || 7 Ulterius dico]Dicoque ulterius L | combinationes]concinationes B | 8 *ante* nominari combinari *del.* E | nominari *legi non potest* V | precessoribus E || 9 *inter* quam *et* plures p *del.* C || 12 unisono]uno sono E || 14 que *sup. lin.* E ||

3

1. Now that these things have been explained, we should proceed to an explanation of intervals.[1] I say that an interval is the combination of two syllables producing a sound consonant or dissonant to the ears; and by "syllables" I understand the musical syllables, of which there are six, ut, re, mi, fa, sol, la.

2. Furthermore, I say that the intervals customarily named in this art by all our predecessors are read out in great number: the unison, the second, the third, the fourth, the fifth, the sixth, the seventh, and the octave, which has the force of the unison, since every song that begins with a unison can also begin with an octave, and vice versa; likewise the ninth, which has the force of the second for the reason stated; the tenth, which, for

---

7-9: . . . the intervals customarily named in this art by all our precedessors are read out in great number and are called by these modern names:[2]

---

[1]Prosdocimo's term for "interval" is *combinatio vocum*--"combination of syllables"--or simply *combinatio*.

[2]In the revision, Prosdocimo indicates that the interval names *secunda, tercia, quarta,* etc., are "modern." He is obviously aware that these terms came to stand alongside the Greek-derived *tonus, ditonus/semiditonus, dyatheseron,* etc., only in the course of the fourteenth century, e.g., in the *Compendium de discantu mensurabili* (1336) of Petrus dictus Palma ociosa (ed. Johannes Wolf, "Ein Beitrag zur Diskantlehre des 14. Jahrhunderts," *Sammelbände der Internationalen Musikgesellschaft* 15 [1913-1914]:504-34), in the treatises *Quilibet affectans* (CS, 3:59a-60a) and *Volentibus introduci* (Version AC [CS, 3:23a-27b]; but in versions E [CS, 3:12a-13b] and Pi [Sachs, *Contrapunctus*, pp. 170-73] the Latin terms stand alone, as in Prosdocimo), and in Goscalcus' *Tractatus de contrapuncto*.

uni tercie assimilatur; et undecima, quarte; et duodecima, quinte; et tercia decima, sexte; et quarta decima, septime; et quinta decima, unisono et octave; et decima sexta, secunde et none; et decima septima, tercie et decime; et decima || octava, quarte et undecime; et decima nona, CS 19 quinte et duodecime; et vigesima, sexte et tercie decime; et vigesima prima, septime et quarte decime; et vigesima secunda, unisono, octave, et quinte decime; et sic ulterius isto modo in infinitum procedendo, si in infinitum voces vel instrumenta elongari possent. Unisonus est quando ambe voces contrapunctum facientes in eadem parte manus musicalis et voce reperte sunt, et dicitur notanter in eadem parte manus musicalis et voce, quoniam possent esse due voces in eadem parte manus musicalis et tamen non unisone, sicut est de fa et mi que in bfa♮mi reperiuntur, que, licet sint in eadem parte manus musicalis, ut apparet, non tamen sunt unisone, quia in eadem voce non sunt nec existere possunt. Secunda est quando una vox in secundo loco manus musicalis a loco alterius reperitur, tercia vero que in tercio, et sic ultra.

---

15 *Huc pertinet emendatio quae in L invenitur:* . . . sicut est de fa et mi que in utroque bfa♮mi reperiuntur . . .

3-4 et decima sexta, secunde et none; et decima septima, tercie *om.* V || 4 *ante* tercie tercie *del.* C || 7 vigesima prima *ex* vigesime prime *alt.* C | *post* decime [[vigesime secunde]] *del.* C || 8 octava V | quinte decime]quintadecime C | sic *sup. lin.* E || 9 infinitum . . . infinitum]infimum . . . infimum B || 10 elongari]augmentari vel elongari L | Unisonus]Unde unisonus L || 12 et voce]ac etiam voce L voce]voces V | *post* sunt no *del.* C | et dicitur *om.* C || 12-13 reperte sunt . . . et voce]reperte sunt . . . et voce, quoniam *in marg.* E || 13 *post* et per *del.* V | et voce]ac etiam voce L || 15 est *om.* C | bfabmi V || 16 ut apparet *om.* L || 17 quia]ut notum est, quoniam L || 18 Secunda]Sed secunda L | quando]quoniam V || 20 que]que est V ||

the reason stated, is considered similar to the third; the eleventh, similar to the fourth; the twelfth, similar to the fifth; the thirteenth, similar to the sixth; the fourteenth, similar to the seventh; the fifteenth, similar to the unison and the octave; the sixteenth, similar to the second and the ninth; the seventeenth, similar to the third and the tenth; the eighteenth, similar to the fourth and the eleventh; the nineteenth, similar to the fifth and the twelfth; the twentieth, similar to the sixth and the thirteenth; the twenty-first, similar to the seventh and the fourteenth; the twenty-second, similar to the unison, the octave, and the fifteenth; and so forth, proceeding in this way to infinity, if the syllables or instruments could be extended to infinity. The unison occurs when both syllables making up the counterpoint are found on the same part of the musical hand and with the same syllable. It is significant that they are said on the same part of the musical hand and with the same syllable, because two syllables could be on the same part of the musical hand and nonetheless not be in unison, like the fa and mi found in bfa♮mi, which, though they be on the same part of the musical hand, as is evident, are nevertheless not in unison, because they are not and cannot exist on the same syllable.[3] The second occurs when one syllable is found in the location on the musical hand second from the first, the third when it is found in the third location, and so forth.

15: . . . like the fa and mi found in either bfa♮mi . . .

---

[3]Prosdocimo's definition of the unison is unusually precise. A more typical definition is that of *Volentibus introduci* (Version AC 1.1; CS, 3:24a): "The unison occurs whenever many notes or syllables are written on the same line or in the same space (Unisonus est quandocumque plures note vel voces invicem collocantur in eadem linea vel spatio)." Prosdocimo points out that this single condition does not suffice: the two notes must also have the same syllable, i.e., chromatic inflection. Ugolino follows Prosdocimo; cf. *Declaratio* 2.4.4 (Seay ed., 2:8).

The medieval gamut, extending from G at the bottom of the bass staff to e" at the top of the treble, was based on interlocking hexachords beginning on G, c, f, g, c', f', and g'. Notes were identified by letter-name and syllable: Γut, Are, Bmi, Cfaut, Dsolre, Elami, Ffaut,

3. Item de istis combinationibus scire debes quod quedam sunt combinationes consonantes sive concordantes sive bonas consonantias auribus humanis resonantes, sicut sunt unisonus, tercia, quinta, sexta, et sibi equivalentes, sicut octava, decima, duodecima, tercia decima, quinta decima, et huiusmodi, et quedam sunt dissonantes sive discordantes sive dissonantias auribus humanis resonantes, sicut sunt secunda, quarta, septima, et sibi equivalentes, uti sunt nona, undecima, quarta decima, et huiusmodi.

3-6 *Huc pertinet emendatio quae in L invenitur:* . . . sicut sunt unisonus, tercia, quedam quinta, sexta, et sibi equivalentes, sicut quedam octava, decima, quedam duodecima, tercia decima, quedam quinta decima, et huiusmodi . . .

---

1 Item]Et L ‖ 3-4 sunt sicut V ‖ 4 sexta]et sexta E | *post* et octava *del.* V ‖ 5 tercia decima]et tercia decima V ‖ 7 discordantes L | dissonantias *om.* C | humanis auribus L ‖ 8 sicut]ut C | sunt *om.* V | septima *legi non potest* L | *post* et sibi [[et sibi]] *del.* C ‖ 9 uti]ut V | nona]nona et L ‖

3. Moreover, concerning these intervals, you ought to know that some intervals are consonant or concordant, producing consonances pleasant to human ears--the unison, the third, the fifth, the sixth, and their equivalents, the octave, the tenth, the twelfth, the thirteenth, the fifteenth, and the like--and some are dissonant or discordant, producing sounds dissonant to human ears--the second, the fourth, the seventh, and their equivalents, the ninth, the eleventh, the fourteenth, and the like.[4] You should

---

3-6: . . . the unison, the third, a certain fifth, the sixth, and their equivalents, a certain octave, the tenth, a certain twelfth, the thirteenth, a certain fifteenth, and the like-- . . .[5]

Gsolreut, alamire, bfa♮mi, csolfaut (i.e., middle C), dlasolre, elami, ffaut, gsolreut, alamire, bfa♮mi, csolfa, dlasol, ela. Each of the two notes called bfa♮mi was peculiar in having its syllables represent different pitches (fa, b flat, written with a round b; mi, b natural, written with a square ♮). Thus it is that b and ♮, though in the same part of the hand (i.e., in the same location on the staff), have different syllables and are not in unison.

[4]The definition of consonance and dissonance on the basis of good or bad sound goes back to Boethius (who, of course, got the idea from the Greeks): "A consonance is the combination of a higher pitch with a lower one, reaching the ears in a pleasant, uniform manner. A dissonance is the combination of two pitches that strikes the ear as rough and unpleasant (Consonantia est acuti soni gravisque mixtura suaviter uniformiterque auribus accidens. Dissonantia vero est duorum sonorum sibimet permixtorum ad aurem veniens aspera atque iniucunda percussio)" (*Musica* 1.8 [*Anicii Manlii Torquati Severini Boetii de institutione arithmetica libri duo, de institutione musica libri quinque*, ed. Gottfried Friedlein (Leipzig: Teubner, 1867; reprint ed., Frankfort: Minerva, 1966), p. 195]). These definitions echo through medieval music theory.

[5]On the significance of the expressions "a certain fifth (quedam quinta)," "a certain octave (quedam octava)," etc., see the emendation to 42.10.

Scias tamen quod quarta et sibi equivalentes minus dissonant quam alie combinationes dissonantes, ymo quodammodo medium tenent inter consonantias veras et dissonantias, in tantum quod secundum quod quidam dicere voluerunt ab antiquis inter consonantias numerabantur.

1-5 *Huc pertinet emendatio quae in L invenitur:* . . . quod quedam quarta et sibi equivalentes, illa scilicet que ex duobus tonis et uno semitonio contexitur, minus dissonant quam alie combinationes dissonantes, ymo quodammodo medium tenent inter puram consonantiam et puram dissonantiam, et aliquantulum ad quintam consonantem et sibi equivalentes tendere videntur, in tantum quod non multum pratici in cantando multotiens assumunt hanc quartam pro una quinta consonante, et propter hoc ab antiquis inter consonantias numerabatur, ac ipsam dyatheseron nominabant, licet alia quarta valde dissonans, que ex tribus tonis componitur atque tritonus nuncupatur, quasi trium tonorum combinatio possit etiam dyatheseron appellari, cum utraque ipsarum ex quatuor vocibus componatur, unde dyatheseron dicitur a dya, quod est de, et theseron, quod est quatuor, et sic combinatio dyatheseron quasi combinatio de quatuor vocibus contexta dicitur.

---

2 quoddammodo E || 4 dicere voluerunt]dicunt E | dicere *om.* C ||

know that the fourth and its equivalents are less dissonant than the other dissonant intervals; in a certain way, indeed, they hold the middle place between true consonances and dissonances--to such a degree that certain of the ancient writers were ready to say that they should be counted among the consonances.[6]

1-5: . . . that a certain fourth--that formed of two whole tones and one semitone--and its equivalents are less dissonant than the other dissonant intervals; in a certain way, indeed, they hold the middle place between pure consonance and pure dissonance and seem to approximate somewhat the consonant fifth and its equivalents--to such a degree that those not much practised in singing frequently take this fourth for the consonant fifth. This is the reason why it was counted among the consonances by the ancients and why they called it *diatessaron*--although the other, exceedingly dissonant, fourth made up of three whole tones and called the tritone (the interval of three whole tones, as it were) could likewise be called *diatessaron*, since either is made up of four syllables. The word *diatessaron* is derived from *dia*, which is "of," and *tessaron*, which is "four," and so the interval of the *diatessaron* is defined as the interval of four syllables, as it were.[7]

---

[6]Many ancient writers developed systems of consonances that included the perfect fourth. Boethius reports such systems that he attributes to Nicomachus, Eubulides, Hippasus, and Ptolemy (*Musica* 1.7, 2.18-19, 5.11-12 [Friedlein ed., pp. 194, 249-51, 360-63]). Macrobius, *Commentarii in somnium Scipionis* 2.1.24 (*Ambrosii Theodosii Macrobii commentarii in somnium Scipionis*, ed. Jacobus Willis [Leipzig: Teubner, 1970], p. 24), and Cassiodorus, *Institutiones* 2.5.7 (*Cassiodori Senatoris institutiones*, ed. R.A.B. Mynors [Oxford: Clarendon Press, 1937], pp. 144-45), transmit similar systems. The fourth was still classified (alongside the fifth) as a medial consonance in thirteenth-century contrapuntal theory, but was excluded from the consonances by theorists of the fourteenth and fifteenth centuries (Sachs, *Contrapunctus*, pp. 57-122).

[7]The discussion of the perfect and augmented fourths in Prosdocimo's revision parallels that in his *Tractatus musice speculative* (D. Raffaello Baralli and Luigi Torri, "Il *Trattato* di Prosdocimo de' Beldomandi contro il *Lucida-*

4. Item sciendum quod combinationum consonantium quedam sunt perfecte et quedam imperfecte. Perfecte sunt sicut unisonus, quinta, et istis || equivalentes, uti sunt CS 19 octava, duodecima, et huiusmodi, et dicuntur perfecte quia perfectissimam consonantiam reddunt auribus humanis; imperfecte vero sunt sicut tercia, sexta, et istis equivalentes, uti sunt decima, tercia decima, et huiusmodi, et dicuntur imperfecte quia, licet consonantiam bonam reddant auribus humanis, non tamen perfectam sed imperfectam.

1-2 *Huc pertinet emendatio quae in L invenitur:* De combinationibus vero consonantibus quedam sunt perfecte et quedam imperfecte. 3-4 *Huc pertinet emendatio quae in L invenitur:* . . . unisonus, quedam quinta, et istis equivalentes, uti sunt quedam octava, quedam duodecima, et huiusmodi, . . . 10 *Huc pertinet emendatio quae in L invenitur:* Et dicitur notanter quandam quintam, quandam octavam, quandam duodecimam, quandam quintam decimam, et huiusmodi esse consonantem, et non dicitur quandam terciam, quandam sextam, et huiusmodi esse consonantem, quoniam, licet omnis tercia et omnis sexta et omnes sibi equivalentes consonantes sint, non tamen omnis quinta nec omnis octava nec omnis duodecima nec omnis quinta decima et huiusmodi dicitur esse consonans, ut inferius habebitur, et ratio huius esse potest quoniam, ex quo huiusmodi consonantes sunt perfecte consonantes, et alie imperfecte consonantes, ut paulo ante habitum est, in geminata est natura has combinationes perfecte consonantes ponere in puncto indivisibili propter sui perfectam consonantiam atque iocunditatem, a quo si recedant discordantes efficiuntur, quod non sic de aliis combinationibus imperfecte consonantibus invenitur, nam earum consonantia non consistit in puncto indivisibili, sed variari potest ipsa adhuc consonantia remanente, ut statim habebitur.

---

1 *post* quod inter *del.* E || 2 Perfecte sunt]sunt V || 3 *post* sicut f *del.* V || 5 quia]quoniam L | reddunt]reddunt sive resonant L || 6 sunt vero C | vero *om.* E | istis]sibi E || 8 quia]quoniam L || 8-9 auribus humanis consonantiam bonam reddant C || 9 reddant]reddant sive resonent L ||

4. It must be known, too, that some of the consonant intervals are perfect and some imperfect. The perfect ones are the unison, the fifth, and their equivalents, the octave, the twelfth, and the like; they are said to be perfect because they produce the consonance most perfect to human ears. The imperfect ones are the third, the sixth, and their equivalents, the tenth, the thirteenth, and the like; they are said to be imperfect because, though they produce a consonance pleasant to human ears, it is not perfect but imperfect.

1-2: Some of the consonant intervals are perfect and some imperfect. 3-4: . . . the unison, a certain fifth, and their equivalents, a certain octave, a certain twelfth, and the like; . . .[8] 10: It is significant that "a certain fifth," "a certain octave," "a certain twelfth," "a certain fifteenth," and the like are said to be consonant, and not that "a certain third," "a certain sixth," and the like are said to be consonant, for though every third, every sixth, and every equivalent interval is consonant, not every fifth, every octave, every twelfth, every fifteenth, or every equivalent interval is said to be consonant, as will be shown below. The reason for this can be that (inasmuch as the consonances of one sort are perfectly consonant, the others imperfectly consonant, as stated a bit earlier) it is inherent in their twin nature to represent the perfectly consonant intervals by indivisible points, on account of their perfect consonance or pleasantness: if they depart from the points, they effect discordant intervals. This is not found to be the case with the other, imperfectly consonant intervals, for their consonance does not consist in indivisible points: rather they can be varied with the consonance remaining,[9] as will straightway be shown.

---

rio di Marchetto da Padova per la prima volta trascritto e illustrato," *Rivista musicale italiana* 20 [1913]:733-34).

[8]On the significance of the expressions "a certain fifth (quedam quinta)," "a certain octave (quedam octava)," and "a certain twelfth (quedam duodecima)," see the emendation to line 10.

[9]I know of no other writer who compares the perfect consonances to indivisible points, but the comparison is apt. Fifths and octaves exist as consonances in only

5. Item sciendum quod duplex reperitur quelibet consonantia preter unisonum, et etiam omnis dissonantia, scilicet maior et minor, sed de dissonantia nullam faciam mentionem quantum ad suam maioritatem vel minoritatem, quoniam nulla dissonantia in contrapuncto proprie sumpto reperiri debet, licet bene in cantu fractibili reperiatur, sed tunc non est cura utrum talis tunc maior vel minor existat. Maior ergo tercia est illa que in se duos continet tonos; minor vero est illa que in se tonum cum semitonio continet. Quinta vero maior est illa que in se tres continet tonos cum uno semitonio, et est illa quinta que inter consonantias perfectas numerata est, et quam dicunt auctores musice in proportione sexquialtera consistere. Quinta vero minor est illa que in se duos continet tonos cum duobus semitoniis, et talis consonans combinatio non est, sed inter

---

7-11 *Huc pertinet emendatio quae in L invenitur:* . . . utrum talis combinatio dissonans in contrapuncto maior vel minor existat. De combinationibus ergo consonantibus sermonem meum prosequendo, et a tercia, prima consonantiarum, unisono dimisso, incipiendo, dico quod tercia maior est illa que in se duos continet tonos, et hec alio nomine ditonus, quasi combinatio duorum tonorum appellatur; tercia vero minor est illa que in se tonum continet cum semitonio, et hec alio nomine semiditonus, quasi combinatio toni cum semitonio, appellatur. Quinta autem maior est illa, que in se tres continet tonos cum uno semitonio, et hec alio nomine dyapente consonans, quasi combinatio consonans de quinque vocibus contexta appellatur, unde dyapente dicitur a dya, quod est de, et pente, quod est quinque, unde dyapente tanquam de quinque sonat, et hec est illa quinta . . .

---

1 Item sciendum]propter quod est sciendum L | reperitur quelibet]est C || 1-2 consonantia]combinatio L || 2 et *om.* CV | et etiam omnis dissonantia *om.* L || 3 dissonantia]combinationibus dissonantibus hic L || 4 vel minoritatem *om.* L || 5 dissonantia]combinatio dissonans L | in contrapuncto *om.* V || 6 *post* tunc talis *del.* B || 8 continet duos B || 9 illa]ista V *ut* 46.3, 4, 6; 82.3; 86.7, 18 | continet]rettinet E || 14 continet duos CE || 15 *post* semitoniis: et nullam in se firmam rettinet proportionem E | et talis consonans combinatio non est]nec consonans combinatio est E et talis combinatio non est consonans L ||

5. It must be known, too, that any consonance save the unison, as well as every dissonance, is found in two inflections, the major and the minor. I shall not mention dissonance with respect to its major or minor inflection, because no dissonance ought to be found in counterpoint construed in the proper sense, though it may well be found in florid melody, but in that case there is no concern whether it exists as major or minor. The major third, then, is that which contains two whole tones, the minor third is that which contains a whole tone with a semitone. The major fifth is that which contains three whole tones with one semitone and is that fifth which is counted among the perfect consonances, and which musical authors define as consisting of the sesquialtera proportion; the minor fifth is that which contains two whole tones with two semitones and is not a consonant interval but is counted

---

7-11: . . . whether the interval dissonant in counterpoint exists as major or minor. To proceed with my discourse on consonant intervals, beginning with the third--the first of the consonances aside from the unison--I assert that the major third is that which contains two whole tones (it is called by another name, ditonus--"the interval of two whole tones," as it were); the minor third is that which contains a whole tone with a semitone (it is called by another name, semiditonus--"the interval of a whole tone with a semitone," as it were). The major fifth is that which contains three whole tones with one semitone (it is called by another name, the consonant *diapente*--"the consonant interval formed of five syllables" as it were. The word *diapente* is derived from *dia*, which is "of," and *pente*, which is "five"; whence *diapente* signifies so much as "of five"), and is that fifth . . .

---

one inflection; if their sizes vary, they become dissonant. Thirds and sixths, on the other hand, can vary between major and minor inflections, still remaining consonant.

combinationes vere discordantes numeratur. Sexta vero maior est illa que in se quatuor continet tonos cum uno semitonio; minor vero sexta est illa que in se tres continet tonos cum duobus semitoniis. Octava maior est illa que in se quinque continet tonos et duo semitonia, et hec est illa octava que inter consonantias perfectas numerata est, et quam auctores musice, antiqui necnon et moderni, in proportione dupla consistere dixerunt. Octava vero minor est illa que in se quatuor || continet tonos cum CS 19
tribus semitoniis, et hec octava inter combinationes vere discordantes numeranda est. Reperitur etiam octava maxima,

---

1-6 *Huc pertinet emendatio quae in L invenitur:* Sexta autem maior est illa que in se quatuor continet tonos cum uno semitonio, et hec alio nomine dyapente consonans cum tono nominatur; sexta vero minor est illa que in se tres continet tonos cum duobus semitoniis, et hec alio nomine dyapente consonans cum semitonio nuncupatur. Octava vero maior est illa que in se quinque continet tonos cum duobus semitoniis, et hec alio nomine dyapason consonans, quasi combinatio consonans de toto consistens appellatur, unde dyapason dicitur a dya, quod est de, et pason, quod est totum, unde dyapason tanquam de toto resonat, et dicitur hec combinatio de toto pro tanto, quoniam ipsa virtualiter in se continet omnes combinationes consonantes, ut clare patet ex hiis que supra habita sunt, nam primo continet in se unisonum, cum sibi similis sit per prius habita; continet etiam in se terciam, quintam, sextam, et se ipsammet octavam, ut clarum est et etiam ab inde supra, cum ab inde supra non sit nisi quedam reiteratio, ut ex hiis que supra habita sunt clarissime patet, et hec est illa octava . . . 10-50.1 *Huc pertinet emendatio quae in L invenitur:* . . . et hec octava inter combinationes vere discordantes numeranda est, et hec gratia exempli reperitur in manu musicali si sumatur fa b acuti contra mi b gravis vel fa b superacuti contra mi b acuti. Reperitur etiam

---

1 discordantes *in marg.* C || 2 quatuor continet *ex* continet quatuor *alt.* B || 3 in se tres *in marg.* B || 4 semitonis C || 5 *post* tonos cum *del.* C || 7 auctores]actiones V | et]in V || 7-8 auctores musice . . . consistere dixerunt]dicunt auctores musice in proportione dupla consistere L || 11 *post* est: nec in se aliquam firmam rettinet proportionem E | etiam *sup. lin.* B ||

among the intervals that are truly discordant. The major sixth is that which contains four whole tones with one semitone, the minor sixth that which contains three whole tones with two semitones. The major octave is that which contains five whole tones and two semitones, and this is that octave which is counted among the perfect consonances, and which musical authors, both ancient and modern, have defined as consisting in the duple proportion; the minor octave is that which contains four whole tones with three semitones, and this octave is to be counted among the truly discordant intervals. An augmented octave is

---

1-6: The major sixth is that which contains four whole tones with one semitone (it is called by another name, the consonant *diapente* with a whole tone), the minor sixth that which contains three whole tones with two semitones (it is designated by another name, the consonant *diapente* with a semitone). The major octave is that which contains five whole tones with two semitones (it is called by another name, the consonant *diapason*--"the consonant interval consisting of the whole," as it were; the word *diapason* is derived from *dia*, which is "of," and *pason*, which is "the whole"; whence *diapason* signifies so much as "of the whole." This interval is said to be "of the whole" since it contains virtually within itself all the consonant intervals, as is clear from what has been learned above: first, it contains the unison, since that interval is similar to it, as learned earlier; it likewise contains the third, the fifth, the sixth, and itself, the octave, as is clear even from the above, since it follows from the above that it is nothing other than a certain repetition, as is perfectly clear from what has been learned above), and this is that octave . . . 10-50.1: . . . and this octave is to be counted among the truly discordant intervals. It is found on the musical hand, for instance, if the fa of high b is taken against the mi of low b or if the fa of very high b is taken against the mi of high b.[10]

---

[10]Prosdocimo classes the notes of the gamut into three registers: low (*graves*), G to g; high (*acute*), a to g'; very high (*superacute*), a' to e"; cf. his *Tractatus musice plane*, B, p. 116ab ("Notandum ulterius quod hee viginti dictiones superius nominate tripartite sunt, quoniam quedam sunt graves, uti sunt octo prime, scilicet a Γut inclusive usque ad primum alamire exclusive, quedam vero acute, uti sunt septem sequentes, scilicet ab alamire

et est illa que in se sex continet tonos et unum semitonium, que octava maxima etiam inter combinationes vere discordantes numeranda est. Et ut brevius et utilius noticia harum vocum combinationum maiorum vel minorum habeatur, notande sunt infrascripte regule.

---

in manu musicali octava maxima, que etiam inter combinationes vere discordantes numeranda est, et est illa que in se sex continet tonos cum uno semitonio, ut verbi gratia si sumatur mi b superacuti contra fa b acuti. Et ut brevius et utilius noticia harum combinationum vocum maiorum vel

---

2-3 discordantes *om.* C ‖ 3 brevis B | noticiam V ‖ 5 infrascripta V ‖

also found, and it is that which contains six whole tones and one semitone; this augmented octave, as well, is to be counted among the truly discordant intervals. In order to gain an understanding of these major and minor intervals more quickly and profitably, the following rules are noted.

An augmented octave, which is likewise to be counted among the truly discordant intervals, is also found on the musical hand, and it is that which contains six whole tones and one semitone--for instance, if mi of very high b is taken against fa of high b.[11] In order to gain an understanding of these major and minor intervals more quickly and profit-

---

primo inclusive usque ad secundum exclusive, relique vero quinque sequentes sunt superacute"). Similar classifications appear in Jacques de Liège, *Speculum musicae* 5.16.10 (*Jacobi Leodiensis speculum musicae*, 7 vols., ed. Roger Bragard, Corpus scriptorum de musica, no. 3 [Rome: American Institute of Musicology, 1955-1973], 5:52); Ugolino, *Declaratio* 1.9-10 (Seay ed., 1:28-30); and Gaffurio, *Practica musicae* 1.1 (Milan, 1496; reprint ed., Farnborough: Gregg, 1967). More commonly, theorists chose not to include G among the low notes, e.g., Guido, *Micrologus* 2 (omitting e") (*Guidonis Aretini micrologus*, ed. Joseph Smits van Waesberghe, Corpus scriptorum de musica, no. 4 [N.p.: American Institute of Musicology, 1955], pp. 93-95); *Introductio musice secundum magistrum de Garlandia* (CS, 1:158a); *Quatuor principalia* 2.5 (CS, 4:208a); Marchetto, *Lucidarium* 14.10-25 (*The "Lucidarium" of Marchetto of Padua: A Critical Edition, Translation, and Commentary*, ed. Jan Herlinger [Chicago: University of Chicago Press, forthcoming]); Walter Odington, *Speculatio* 5.1.14-17 (omitting e") (*Walteri Odington summa de speculatione musicae*, ed. Frederick F. Hammond, Corpus scriptorum de musica, no. 14 [N.p.: American Institute of Musicology, 1970], pp. 92-93); Legrense, *Vera quamque facilis ad cantandum atque brevis introductio* (CS, 4:346a); Johannes Tinctoris, *Dictionary of Musical Terms*, ed. Carl Parrish (Glencoe: Free Press, 1963), pp. 6-7, 34-35, 60-61; Tinctoris, *Expositio manus* 1.30 (G classed as "lowest" [*gravissima*]) (*Johannis Tinctoris opera theoretica*, 1:35); Burzio, *Florum libellus* 1.16 (Massera ed., p. 86).

Thus the intervals Prosdocimo designates here are those between b♭ and B♮ and between b♭' and b♮.

[11]I.e., b♮' against b♭.

6. Prima ergo regula est hec, quod quantitas discreta in se comprehendens tonos et semitonia in istis combinationibus vocum tam concordantibus quam discordantibus reperta in eodem numero consistit a quo denominata est combinatio illa, una unitate dempta, ut verbi gratia si de numero binario, a quo denominata est secunda, subripiatur unitas, remanet unitas alia, que est quantitas tonorum sive semitoniorum in secunda repertorum, quia secunda non habet nisi tonum aut semitonium unum. Similiter si de numero ternario, a quo denominata est tercia, removeatur unitas, remanet numerus binarius, qui est quantitas tonorum et semitoniorum in tercia repertorum, quia tercia non habet nisi duos tonos vel tonum cum semitonio. Similiter si de numero quaternario, a quo denominata est quarta, removeatur unitas, remanet numerus ternarius, qui est quantitas tonorum et semitoniorum in quarta repertorum, quoniam quarta non habet nisi tres tonos vel duos cum uno semitonio. Similiter si de numero quinario, a quo denominata est quinta, removeatur unitas, remanet numerus quaternarius, qui est quantitas tonorum et semitoniorum in quinta repertorum, quia quinta non habet nisi tres tonos cum uno semitonio vel duos tonos

---

minorum habeatur, notande sunt infrascripte regule, quarum prima est hec, quod quantitas discreta . . .

---

1 quantitas discreta]quantitas discreta sive numeralis L || 2 comprehendens]insimul comprehendens L || 2-3 vocum combinationibus L || 3 tam]quam V || 4-5 illa combinatio L || 5 dempta]remota L || 6 subripiatur]removeatur L || 7 alia unitas L || 7-8 semitonorum B semitorum V || 8 secunda (*sec.*)]a secunda C || 8-9 non habet nisi . . . semitonium unum]non continet in se nisi unum tonum aut unum semitonium L || 9 semitonum V || 10 removetur V || 11 quantitas L | semitonorum BV || 12 tercia repertorum L | *post* nisi to *del.* B || 12-13 non habet nisi . . . tonum cum semitonio]non continet in se nisi duos tonos aut tonum unum cum uno semitonio L || 12-16 in tercia repertorum . . . semitoniorum *om.* C || 16 semitonorum BV || 17 habet]continet in se L | vel]aut L | cum]et C || 18 *post* quinta [[removeatur quantitas removet]] *del.* C || 20 semitonorum BV || 21 habet]continet in se L | *post* habet [[non habet]] *del.* C | *post* semitonio quia *del.* C ||

6. The first rule is this: that the discrete quantity[12] of whole tones and semitones found in these intervals, concordant and discordant, consists of the same number by which that interval is named, less one. For example, if from the number 2, by which the second is named, 1 is subtracted, another 1 remains--which is the quantity of whole tones or semitones found in the second, because the second has nothing other than one whole tone or semitone. Similarly, if from the number 3, by which the third is named, 1 is removed, the number 2 remains--which is the quantity of whole tones and semitones found in the third, because the third has nothing other than two whole tones or a whole tone with a semitone. Similarly, if from the number 4, by which the fourth is named, 1 is removed, the number 3 remains--which is the quantity of whole tones and semitones found in the fourth, because the fourth has nothing other than three whole tones or two with one semitone. Similarly, if from the number 5, by which the fifth is named, 1 is removed, the number 4 remains--which is the quantity of whole tones and semitones found in the fifth, because the fifth has nothing other than three whole tones with one semitone or two

---

ably, the following rules are noted, of which the first is this: that the discrete quantity . . .

---

[12]"Discrete quantity" is number. Boethius defines the two sorts of quantity in *Musica* 2.3 (Friedlein ed., p. 228): "Every quantity, according to Pythagoras, is either continuous or discrete. That which is continuous is called magnitude; that which is discrete, multitude. (Omnis vero quantitas secundum Pythagoram vel continua vel discreta est. Sed quae continua est, magnitudo appellatur, quae discreta est, multitudo)."

cum duobus semitoniis; et sic per simile de omnibus aliis vocum combinationibus, tam concordantibus quam discordantibus. || CS 1

7. Secunda regula est hec, et, per simile, comunis ad omnes vocum combinationes tam concordantes quam discordantes, quod omnis vocum combinatio maior ab unisono exclusive usque ad quintam exclusive reperta in se nullum continet semitonium; minor vero unicum solum in se continere semitonium inventa est. Omnis vero maior vocum combinatio a quinta inclusive usque ad octavam exclusive reperta in se unicum solum continet semitonium; minor vero duo semitonia in se continere reperta est. Omnis vero maior vocum combinatio ab octava inclusive usque ad duodecimam exclusive reperta in se duo continet semitonia; minor vero tria. Omnis vero maior vocum combinatio a duodecima inclusive usque ad quintam decimam exclusive reperta tria in se continet semitonia; minor vero quatuor. Et sic deinceps, semper de combinatione perfecta in combinationem perfectam sibi immediatam unicum solum semitonium addendo;

6-8 *Huc pertinet emendatio quae in L invenitur:* . . . omnis vocum maior combinatio ab unisono exclusive, qui non dicitur maior nec minor, usque ad quintam exclusive reperta in se nullum continet semitonium; . . . 18-54.2 *Huc pertinet emendatio quae in L invenitur:* . . . semper de combinatione consonante perfecta in combinationem consonantem perfectam sequentem et sibi immediatam unicum solum semitonium superaddendo; et dicitur maior combinatio quia

---

1 *post* sic de *del.* E | per simile]per similem V || 3 *post* discordantibus: est prosequendum L || 4 *post* hec quod *del.* B || 5-6 combinationes . . . vocum *om.* V || 8 unicum *ex* unum *alt.* E | continere *ex* rettinet *alt.* E || 9 inventa est *in marg.* E || 10 a quinta]ab octava C | ad octavam]ad duodecimam C || 11 solum]sonum V | minor]nunca V || 12 semitonia]semitoū (=?) V | se *om.* V | vero]autem L || 14 *post* continet fe *del.* E || 15 Omnis vero]Sed omnis L || 16 quintadecimam C | *post* reperta [[a se]] *del.* V || 18 semper de]a C | *post* perfecta [[usque ad]] *del.* C || 19 perfectam *ex* imperfectam *alt.* E | sibi *sup. lin.* E | solum]sonum V | addendo semitonium E ||

whole tones with two semitones; and thus similarly for all other intervals, concordant and discordant.

7. The second rule is this (and similarly, common to all intervals, concordant and discordant): that every major interval found between the unison and the fifth (excluding both these) contains no semitone; the minor interval is found to contain only a single semitone. Every major interval found between the fifth and the octave (including the fifth but excluding the octave) contains only a single semitone; the minor interval is found to contain two semitones. Every major interval found between the octave and the twelfth (including the octave but excluding the twelfth) contains two semitones, every minor interval three. Every major interval found between the twelfth and the fifteenth (including the twelfth but excluding the fifteenth) contains three semitones, every minor interval four; and so on, always adding only a single semitone from perfect interval to the very next perfect interval.

6-8: . . . every major interval found between the unison (which is said to be neither major nor minor) and the fifth (excluding both these) contains no semitone; . . .
18-54.2: . . . always adding only a single semitone from perfect consonant interval to the very next and sequential perfect consonant interval. An interval is said to be

et dicitur maior combinatio quia per maiorem distantiam dilatatur, minor vero quia per minorem.

8. Tercia regula est hec, quod quelibet combinatio maior ipsammet combinationem minorem excedit per semitonium maius, ex quo sequitur quod in reducendo maiorem combinationem ad ipsammet minorem vel e contra non oportet nisi addere vel diminuere tale semitonium maius.

9. Quarta et ultima regula est hec, quod omnia semitonia in combinationibus reperta sunt semitonia minora,

---

per maiorem distantiam dilatatur una vox illius combinationis ab alia quam dilatetur in alia eiusdem speciei et eiusdem partis manus musicalis, et ideo hec alia combinatio minor nuncupatur quia per minorem distantiam voces in ipsa dilatantur respectu prioris iam dicte. 8-56.3 *Huc pertinet emendatio quae in L invenitur:* . . . omnia semitonia in combinationibus reperta sunt minora semitonia, licet Marchetus, michi concivis paduanus, velit oppositum in suo Lucidario, ut ibi videri habet ubi ponit tria genera

---

4 ipsammet combinationem]se ipsammet L || 4-5 semitonium maius]semitonium dyatonicum, quod maius semitonium apud musicos appellatur E || 5 in *sup. lin.* B || 7 di *ex* diminuere *sup. lin.* C | semitonium maius]semitonium maius sive dyatonicum E || 9 *post* semitonia [[i mira]] *del.* C | semitonia minora]semitonia enarmonica, que apud musicos semitonia minora nuncupantur E ||

An interval is said to be major because it is extended over a greater distance, minor because it is extended over a lesser.

8. The third rule is this: that any major interval exceeds the same minor interval by a major semitone;[13] from which it follows that in reducing a major interval to its minor form, or vice versa, it is necessary only to add or subtract a major semitone.

9. The fourth and last rule is this: that all semitones found in intervals are minor semitones. An investiga-

---

major because one syllable of the interval is extended over a greater distance from the other syllable than it is in the other interval of the same species and in the same location on the musical hand, and the other interval is called minor because its syllables are extended over a lesser distance with respect to those of the other interval already mentioned. 8-56.3: . . . all semitones found in intervals are minor semitones--though Marchetto, my fellow Paduan citizen, claims the opposite in his *Lucidarium*,[14] as is seen where he posits that three genera of

---

[13]For "major semitone (semitonium maius)" ms. E has "the diatonic semitone, which musicians call the major semitone (semitonium diatonicum, quod maius semitonium apud musicos appellatur)." The term "diatonic semitone" was coined by Marchetto of Padua (see the Introduction, note 7 [pp. 9-11]). Prosdocimo objects to its use (see the *Tractatus musice speculative* [Baralli and Torri ed., p. 752] and the revision of *Contrapunctus* 3.9 [pp. 54.8-56.3]), and its appearance in a redaction of one of his own treatises confirms his testimony that Marchetto's "errors," as he calls them, had spread throughout Italy (Prosdocimo speaks of the "errores huius marcheti per totam ytaliam . . . diuulgatos," *Tractatus musice speculative* [Baralli and Torri ed., p. 731]). Ms. E, in attributing the term "major semitone" to the "musicians"--i.e., theorists--(and the term "diatonic semitone" implicitly to "singers"--practicing musicians), confirms Prosdocimo's report that Marchetto's theories were held to be accurate by performers but not theorists ("uerissimos a cantoribus non tamen musicis reputatos" [ibid.]).

Similar variants appear elsewhere in E.

[14]On Marchetto's semitones, see the Introduction, note 7 (pp. 9-11). Prosdocimo's emendation incorporates

quorum semitoniorum, tam maiorum quam minorum, investigatio ad propositum non spectat, sed solius theorici musici est speculatio, cum simplex praticus propter quid rei inquirere non debet sed ad solum quia est rei debet contentus permanere. || CS 19

---

semitoniorum in diversis locis manus musicalis et diversis cantibus usitanda, sed sibi in hoc fides non est adhibenda, eo quod, non theoricus sed simplex praticus, scribere voluit de hiis que totaliter ignoravit. Divisit nanque tonum in quinque partes equales, quod est impossibile, ut videri habet in theorica musice per me compilata, et nominavit quamlibet illarum quinque partium hoc nomine, dyesis, totaliter ignorans quid apud auctores musice, ut Boetium et alios, importet hoc nomen, dyesis. Voluitque ulterius duas dyeses quoddam semitonium componere apud ipsum semitonium enarmonicum appellatum, tres vero dyeses aliud semitonium componere apud ipsum semitonium dyatonicum nuncupatum, quatuor vero dyeses aliud semitonium componere apud ipsum semitonium cromaticum nominatum, ignorans etiam totaliter quid auctores musice intelligant per ista tria nomina, scilicet enarmonicum, dyatonicum, et cromaticum, cum per ipsa intelligant tria diversa genera tetracordorum [*ms.*: tetarcordorum], et non semitoniorum, ut ipse voluit. Semitonia nanque secundum musice auctores et secundum toni divisionem in duo inequalia solum duo reperiuntur, scilicet maius et minus, et non tria, maius, scilicet, medium, atque minus, ut ipse voluit, sed ipsa investigare non est presentis speculationis, sed solius theorici musici est speculatio, . . .

---

2 solius]sollus C || 4 debeat E | ad solum quia est rei]solum ad ipsius rei quia est L ||

tion of these semitones, major and minor, is not apposite to the matter at hand, but is the province of the musical theorist alone; the simple performer ought not to inquire after the wherefore of the thing, but ought to remain content with the what.

---

semitones are to be used in different locations on the musical hand and in different melodies. In this matter he is not to be trusted, because, not a theorist but a simple performer, he purposed to write concerning things of which he was totally ignorant. He divided the whole tone into five equal parts--which is impossible, as is seen in the theory of music I compiled--and called any of these five parts by the term, diesis, totally ignoring what this term, diesis, implies to musical authors like Boethius and others. He further claimed that two dieses make up a certain semitone he called the enharmonic semitone, three dieses another semitone he designated as the diatonic semitone, and four dieses another semitone he called the chromatic semitone, again, totally ignoring how musical authors understand these three terms, enharmonic, diatonic, and chromatic, for they understand them as three different genera of tetrachords--not semitones, as he maintained. According to musical authors and according to the division of the whole tone into two unequal parts, there are found only two semitones, the major and the minor, and not three, the major, the middle, and the minor, as he maintained. But it is not part of the present inquiry to investigate these matters. It is the province of the musical theorist alone; . . .

---

extracts from his *Tractatus musice speculative* (Baralli and Torri ed., pp. 731, 752).

4

1. Pro ordinatione autem harum combinationum in contrapuncto proprie sumpto has nota regulas.

2. Prima ergo regula est hec, quod discordantie superius nominate, scilicet secunda, quarta, septima, quinta minor, octava minor et maxima, et sibi equivalentia, nullo modo in contrapuncto usitande sunt, eo quod propter ipsarum dissonantiam cordialiter armonie et nature inimicantur, que finis huius artis existere videtur; usitantur tamen in cantu fractibili, eo quod in ipso propter velocitatem vocum earum non sentiuntur dissonantie.

3. Secunda regula est hec, quod contrapunctus nunquam incipi vel finiri debet nisi in combinationibus perfectis, scilicet in unisono vel in quinta maiori vel octava maiori vel in hiis equivalentibus, et ratio huius est quoniam

---

5-9 *Huc pertinet emendatio quae in L invenitur:* . . . nullo modo in contrapuncto proprie sumpto usitande sunt, eo quod propter ipsarum dissonantiam cordialiter armonie et nature inimicantur, que armonia huius artis finis est; usitantur tamen in cantu fractibili, . . . 11-13 *Huc pertinet emendatio quae in L invenitur:* . . . quod contrapunctus proprie sumptus semper incipi et finiri debet in vocum combinationibus consonantibus perfectis, sicut in unisono . . .

---

1 *Tit.*: Capitulum secundum, De ordinatione combinationum *fort. m. sec.* E | combinationum]combinationum vocum L || 3 hec est E | discordantia V || 4 *post* quarta quinta *del.* C | *post* septima: et E || 5 et(*pr.*)]atque L || 10 earum] istarum combinationum L || 11 *post* contrapunctus non *del.* C || 12 finiri vel incipi E || 13 octava maiori]in octava maiori ELV || 14 hiis equivalentibus]equivalentibus istis L ||

4

1. For the ordering of these intervals in counterpoint construed in the proper sense, note these rules.

2. The first rule is this: that the discords named above--the second, the fourth, the seventh, the minor fifth, the minor and augmented octaves, and their equivalents--are not used in counterpoint in any way,[1] because, on account of their dissonance, they are deeply hostile to harmony and nature, which seem to be the end of this art. They are used in florid melody, however, because there, on account of the speed of their syllables, the dissonances are not perceived.

3. The second rule is this: that counterpoint ought to begin and end only with perfect intervals--with the unison, the major fifth, the major octave, and their equivalents;[2] the reason for this is if the listener is to

---

5-9: . . . are not used in counterpoint construed in the proper sense in any way, because, on account of their dissonance, they are deeply hostile to harmony and nature, which harmony is the end of this art. They are used in florid melody, however, . . . 11-13: . . . that counterpoint construed in the proper sense ought always to begin and end with perfectly consonant intervals--with the unison, . . .

---

[1]Prosdocimo's rules are of the sort found frequently in the fourteenth and fifteenth centuries. For rule 1, cf. Petrus dictus Palma ociosa, *Compendium* (Wolf ed., pp. 508, 518); *Quatuor principalia* 4.2.20 (CS, 4:281a); *Volentibus introduci*, Version AC 3.1 (CS, 3:27a), Version Pi (Sachs, *Contrapunctus*, p. 173); Ugolino, *Declaratio* 2.3.36 (Seay ed., 2:7); Tinctoris, *Liber de arte contrapuncti* 2.23 (Seay ed., 2:121-24); Burzio, *Florum libellus* 2.1.13-14 (Massera ed., p. 118).

[2]Most fourteenth- and fifteenth-century counterpoint

si auditor per armonias mulceri habet, oportet ipsum primitus admoveri per armonias dulciores et nature amicabiliores, que sunt consonantie perfecte superius nominate, et sic ipse preponende sunt. Demum etiam ipse auditor dimitti debet cum dulcore et armonia nature delectabili, ne ipsius auditoris anima dulci consonantia precedente mota duritie consonantie finalis ab eo quod per armoniam intenditur, scilicet gaudio et delectatione, amoveatur.

4. Tercia regula est hec, quod insimul cum cantu supra vel infra quem contrapunctamus nunquam ascendere vel descendere debemus cum eadem combinatione perfecte concordante, ut cum unisono vel quinta maiori vel octava maiori vel cum hiis equivalentibus, licet bene cum diversis vocum combinationibus perfecte concordantibus hoc agere

---

1 habeat L | ipsum]ipsam V || 2 d *ex* admoveri *sup. lin.* E | amicabiles V || 4 etiam *om.* V || 5 armonie L || 7 *post* per a *del.* B || 8 delectatione *ex* delectationem *alt.* E | amoveatur]removeatur L || 9 *post* quod si *del.* B || 10 quem]quam V || 12 *post* quinta concordante *del.* C || 13 cum (*pr.*) *om.* C | hiis]istis L || 14 combinationibus vocum L ||

be charmed by these harmonies, he should at first be moved by the harmonies that are sweeter and more amicable by nature; these are the perfect consonances named above, and thus they are to be placed first. Finally, the listener ought to be sent away with the sweetness and harmony delectable to nature, lest the listener's spirit, moved by the sweet preceding consonance, be repelled by the harshness of the final consonance from that toward which harmony is directed, enjoyment and delight.

4. The third rule is this: that we ought never to ascend or descend in identical perfectly concordant intervals with the melody above or below which we make counterpoint--in a unison or a major fifth or a major octave or in their equivalents--though we may well do so in different perfectly concordant intervals.[3] The reason

---

treatises agree with Prosdocimo's rule, e.g., *Quatuor principalia* 4.2.20-21 (CS, 4:281ab); *Quilibet affectans* (CS, 3:60a); *Volentibus introduci*, Versions AC 3.1 (CS, 3:27a), E (CS, 3:12b), Pi (Sachs, *Contrapunctus*, p. 171); *Cum notum sit* (CS, 3:62ab); Antonius de Leno, *Regulae de contrapuncto* (CS, 3:308b); Ramos, *Musica practica* 2.1.1 (*Musica practica Bartolomei Rami de Pareia*, ed. Johannes Wolf, Publikationen der Internationalen Musikgesellschaft, Beihefte, vol. 2 [Leipzig: Breitkopf und Härtel, 1901], p. 65); Hothby, *Regulae contrapuncti* 2-4, *Regule dil contrapunto* [2.]2, *Regulae Hothbi supra contrapunctum* 6, *Spetie tenore del contrapunto prima* 3 (Johannes Hothby, *De arte contrapuncti*, ed. Gilbert Reaney, Corpus scriptorum de musica, no. 26 [Neuhausen-Stuttgart: American Institute of Musicology, Hänssler, 1977], pp. 63, 75, 101, 81); Burzio, *Florum libellus* 2.3.18-19 (Massera ed., p. 119); Guilielmus Monachus, *Praecepta* 6 (*Guilielmi Monachi de preceptis artis musicae*, ed. Albert Seay, Corpus scriptorum de musica, no. 11 [N.p.: American Institute of Musicology, 1965], p. 34). Others allow an imperfect consonance at the beginning, e.g., Jacques de Liège, *Speculum musicae* 7.5.21 (Bragard ed., 7:14); Goscalcus, *Tractatus de contrapuncto* (Ellsworth ed., 1:33); Gaffurio, *Practica musicae* 3.3. Ugolino, *Declaratio* 2.6.2-4 (Seay ed., 2:12), demands a perfect consonance at the end but states no conditions about the beginning. Tinctoris, *Liber de arte contrapuncti* 3.1 (Seay ed., 2:146), allows an imperfect consonance at the beginning if the piece begins with a rest.

[3]This is the cardinal rule of counterpoint in the fourteenth and fifteenth centuries. Cf. Petrus dictus Palma ociosa, *Compendium* (Wolf ed., p. 507); *Quatuor princi-*

possumus, et ratio huius est quoniam idem cantaret unus quod alter, dato quod in || diversis vocibus insimul concordantiam habentibus, quod contrapuncti non est intentio, cum eius intentio sit quod illud quod ab uno cantatur diversum sit ab illo quod ab altero pronuntiatur, et hoc per concordantias bonas et debite ordinatas. CS 19

5. Quarta regula est hec, quod contrapunctare non debemus cum vocum combinationibus imperfecte concordantibus continue, nullam combinationem perfecte consonantem interponendo, quoniam tunc ita durum esset hoc cantare, quod in ipso nulla penitus repperiretur armonia, que armonia finis totalis musice existere videtur.

6. Quinta regula est hec, quod in combinationibus perfecte consonantibus nunquam ponere debemus mi contra fa, nec e contra, quoniam statim ipsas vocum combinationes

---

11-12 *Huc pertinet emendatio quae in L invenitur:* . . . que armonia finis est totalis musice.

---

1 cantaret unus]cantaretur C || 2 alter]cantaret alter L || 3 *post* est ratio *del.* B || 4 quod (*sec.*) *alt. ex verb. illeg.* E || 6 per]pro V || 11 reperiri V ||

for this is that one voice would sing the same as the other (granted, with different syllables concordantly related), which is not the purpose of counterpoint; its purpose is that what is sung by one voice be different from what is pronounced by the other, and that this be done through concords that are good and properly ordered.[4]

5. The fourth rule is this: that we ought not continually to make counterpoint with imperfectly concordant intervals without inserting any perfectly consonant intervals,[5] because it would then be hard to sing; for no harmony whatever would be found in the counterpoint, and harmony seems to be the end of all music.

6. The fifth rule is this: that in perfectly consonant intervals we ought never to place mi against fa or vice versa,[6] because we would straightway make the perfectly

---

11-12: . . . and harmony is the end of all music.

---

palia 4.2.11, 20 (CS, 4:278a, 281a); *Quilibet affectans* (CS, 3:60a); *Cum notum sit* (CS, 3:61ab); *Volentibus introduci*, Version AC 3.1 (CS, 3:27a), E (CS, 3:12b), Pi (Sachs, *Contrapunctus*, p. 171); Goscalcus, *Tractatus de contrapuncto* (Ellsworth ed., 1:32); Ugolino, *Declaratio* 2.25.15 (Seay ed., 2:31); Tinctoris, *Liber de arte contrapuncti* 3.2 (Seay ed., 2:147-48); Ramos, *Practica musicae* 2.1.1 (Wolf ed., pp. 65-66); Hothby, *Regulae contrapuncti* 15, *Regule dil contrapuncto* 5, *Regulae Hothbi* 11, *Spetie tenore* 6 (Reaney ed., pp. 64, 74, 101, 83); Burzio, *Florum libellus* 2.3.22, 24 (Massera ed., p. 120); Gaffurio, *Musica practica* 3.3; Guilielmus Monachus, *Praecepta* 6 (Seay ed., p. 34). Tinctoris reports that some allow parallel perfect concords separated by a rest, Gaffurio (with disapproval) that some allow parallel fifths if one is diminished.

[4]Prosdocimo's dictum that the melodies be different recalls traditional definitions of counterpoint, e.g., *Quatuor principalia* 4.2.11 (CS, 4:278a): "Discant is the consonance of some *different* melodies (Discantus est aliquorum *diversorum* cantuum consonantia)."

[5]For similar statements, see *Quatuor principalia* 4.2.20 (CS, 4:281b); *Volentibus introduci*, Version AC 3.1 (CS, 3:27a), Pi 10-11 (Sachs, *Contrapunctus*, p. 171); *Cum notum sit* (CS, 3:61b); Ugolino, *Declaratio* 2.25.19 (Seay ed., 2:31).

[6]For similar statements, see Antonius de Leno, *Regulae de contrapuncto* (CS, 3:309a); Ugolino, *Declaratio*

perfecte consonantes minores vel maximas constitueremus, que discordantes sunt, ut supra dictum est.

7. Sexta et ultima regula est hec, quod cum combinationibus imperfecte consonantibus, maioribus sive minoribus, ascendere vel descendere possumus insimul cum cantu supra vel infra quem contrapunctamus, combinationes tamen perfecte concordantes aliquando interponendo, cuius ratio est quia ex hoc insurgit cantus diversus et non idem propter ineptitudinem quam habet natura ad has combinationes imperfecte

---

3-6 *Huc pertinet emendatio quae in L invenitur:* . . . quod cum combinationibus imperfecte consonantibus, maioribus sive minoribus, eisdem vel diversis, ascendere vel descendere possumus insimul cum cantu supra vel infra quem contrapunctamus, . . . 8-66.2 *Huc pertinet emendatio quae in L invenitur:* . . . ex hoc insurgit cantus diversus et non idem ac tamen cum armonia et delectabilis, et si diceres quare non apparet ita idem cantus in diversis vocibus quando ascendimus vel descendimus insimul cum cantu supra vel infra quem contrapunctamus cum eisdem combinationibus vocum imperfecte consonantibus, sicut apparet idem cantus in diversis vocibus quando ascendimus vel descendimus insimul cum cantu supra vel infra quem contrapunctamus cum eisdem vocum combinationibus perfecte consonantibus, ad hoc dico quod hoc ideo est, quia natura non apprehendit illud esse unum et idem in combinationibus imperfecte

---

1 constituiremus B constituerimus C || 3-4 cum combinationibus]cumbinationibus V || 5 *post* insimul [[vel infra]] *del.* C || 6 quem]quam V || 7 concordantes]consonantes L | aliquando *in marg.* E || 8 consurgit E || 9 natura *ex* naturam *alt.* C ||

consonant intervals minor or augmented, which forms are discordant, as was said above.

7. The sixth and last rule is this: that we may ascend or descend in major or minor intervals imperfectly consonant with the melody above or below which we make counterpoint, occasionally inserting perfectly concordant intervals.[7] The reason for this is that from this procedure arises a different melody--not identical to the other--on account of the lack of conformity that nature has in these

---

3-6 . . . that we may ascend or descend in major or minor intervals, identical or different, imperfectly consonant with the melody above or below which we make counterpoint, . . . 8-66.2: . . . from this procedure arises a different melody--not identical to the other--though the harmony is nonetheless delightful. If you should ask why the same melody does not appear in different syllables when we ascend or descend in identical imperfectly consonant intervals with the melody above or below which we make counterpoint (as the same melody does appear in different syllables when we ascend or descend in identical perfectly consonant intervals with the melody above or below which we make counterpoint), I assert that this is so because nature does not perceive a melody in imperfectly consonant intervals to be one and the same on account of the lack

---

2.25.22-23 (Seay ed., 2:31); Tinctoris, *Liber de arte contrapuncti* 2.23.1-4 (Seay ed., 2:143); Hothby, *Regule dil contrapunto* 7, *Spetie tenore* 10 (Reaney ed., pp. 74, 85); Guilielmus Monachus, *Praecepta* 6 (Seay ed., p. 35).

[7]For similar provisions allowing parallel imperfect consonances, see Petrus dictus Palma ociosa, *Compendium* (Wolf ed., p. 507); *Volentibus introduci*, Version AC 3.1 (CS, 3:26b-27b), E (CS, 3:12b), Pi (Sachs, *Contrapunctus*, p. 171); Tinctoris, *Liber de arte contrapuncti* 3.2.2-7 (Seay ed., 2:147-48); Ramos, *Musica practica* 2.1.1 (Wolf ed., pp. 65-66); Hothby, *Regulae contrapuncti* 15, *Regule dil contrapuncto* 5, *Spetie tenore* 5 (Reaney ed., pp. 64, 74, 83); Guilielmus Monachus, *Praecepta* 6 (Seay ed., p. 34). Some treatises explicitly allow two or three parallel imperfect consonances: *Quatuor principalia* 4.2.20 (CS, 4:281b); Ugolino, *Declaratio* 2.25.17-18 (Seay ed., 2:31); Burzio, *Florum libellus* 2.25 (Massera ed., p. 120). Others allow two, three, or four: *Quilibet affectans* (CS, 3:60a); Goscalcus, *Tractatus de contrapuncto* (Ellsworth ed., 1:32).

consonantes, ac tamen cum armonia et delectabilis, unde scire debes quod inter quaslibet duas consonantias perfectas immediatas cadit una imperfecta, ut verbi gratia inter unisonum et quintam cadit tercia, inter vero quintam et octavam cadit sexta, inter vero octavam et duodecimam cadit decimam, et sic ulterius. Et quando fit accessus ab aliqua istarum consonantiarum imperfectarum ad aliquam perfectarum inter quas ipsa imperfecta combinatio ponitur fit dulcissimus modus cantandi. Reperiuntur etiam et

---

consonantibus propter ineptitudinem quam ipsa habet ad has combinationes imperfecte consonantes, unde, si bene consideramus, natura magis comprehendit idem in contrapunctando solum cum octavis consonantibus quam in contrapunctando solum cum quintis consonantibus, quod non est nisi quia maiorem consonantiam habet natura in octavis consonantibus quam in quintis consonantibus, cum sit consonantia consonantiarum si sic est, ergo non est mirandum si natura non apprehendat idem in contrapunctando solum cum eisdem vocum combinationibus imperfecte consonantibus, cum in ipsis multo minus ipsa natura delectetur quam in quintis concordantibus, ut clarum est. Sed si quandoque inter istas combinationes imperfecte consonantes interponantur combinationes perfecte consonantes fit dulcis armonia atque delectabilis, ut in regula habetur, propter quod sciendum quod . . . 5-6 *Huc pertinet emendatio quae in L invenitur:* . . . inter autem octavam et duodecimam cadit decima, sed inter duodecimam et quintam decimam cadit tercia decima, et sic ulterius. 9-68.5 *Huc pertinet emendatio quae in L invenitur:* . . . fit dulcissimus modus cantandi, sicut de tercia ad unisonum vel quintam et de sexta ad quintam vel octavam, et sic de aliis. Reperiuntur etiam tamen multi alii diversi modi cantandi ab istis

---

1 ac tamen]*fort.* actum BCV || 3 immediatas]sibi invicem immediatas L | imperfecta]combinatio imperfecta L | verbi gratia]gratia exempli C || 8 combinatio imperfecta L ||

imperfectly consonant intervals--though the harmony is nonetheless delightful. Hence you ought to know that between any two successive perfect consonances there should fall an imperfect one. For instance, between a unison and a fifth there should fall a third, between a fifth and an octave there should fall a sixth, between an octave and a twelfth there should fall a tenth, and so forth. When an approach is made from one of these imperfect consonances to some one of the perfect ones among which the imperfect interval is placed, there results an extremely charming style of singing.[8] There are other extremely

---

of conformity nature has in these imperfectly consonant intervals. So--if we consider the matter carefully we see that nature grasps the identity more completely when counterpoint is made with consonant octaves exclusively than when it is made with consonant fifths exclusively; this is because nature has greater consonance in consonant octaves than in consonant fifths because the consonance of the consonant intervals is as it is. It is therefore no wonder that nature does not perceive identity when counterpoint is made with identical imperfectly consonant intervals exclusively, for nature delights in these much less than in concordant fifths, as is clear. But if perfectly consonant intervals are inserted now and then among the imperfectly consonant intervals, a sweet-sounding, delightful harmony results, as stated by the rule. On this account, it must be known that . . . 4-6: . . . between an octave and a twelfth there should fall a tenth, between a twelfth and a fifteenth there should fall a thirteenth, and so forth. 9-68.5: . . . there results an extremely charming style of singing--from a third to a unison or a fifth, from a sixth to a fifth or an octave, and so forth. There are many other styles of singing

---

[8]The same sorts of progressions Prosdocimo recommends are favored also by Ugolino, *Declaratio* 2.25.20-21 (Seay ed., 2:31), and Guilielmus Monachus, *Praecepta* 6 (Seay ed., pp. 34-35). *Regulae Hothbi* 16-24 (Reaney ed., p. 102); Ramos, *Musica practica* 2.1.1 (Wolf ed., p. 67); and Burzio, *Florum libellus* 2.3.29 (Massera ed., pp. 121-22) recommend that imperfect consonances move to perfect ones through stepwise contrary motion. The last two seem to admit oblique motion also.

alii modi dulcissimi cantandi, quos scribere foret valde
difficile et forte im||possibile, cum tales modi quodammodo CS 198
infiniti sint, et diversis diversimode delectabiles, qua
propter insurgit diversitas componentium, et ideo a scriptura relinquendi.

---

et etiam inter se, quos scribere foret valde difficile et forte impossibile, eo quod tales diversi modi cantandi quodammodo infiniti sunt, et diversis diversimode delectabiles, qua propter insurgit diversitas componentium, et quia intellectus noster infinita capere non potest, cum non sit infinite capacitatis sed finite, eo quod aliter in hoc intellectui divino adequaretur, quod non est dicendum. Pro tanto huiusmodi modi a scriptura relinquendi sunt, nec adhuc scribi possent propter sui infinitatem.

---

1 dulcissimi modi C | foret]fieret C ||

charming styles of singing to be found; to write them down would be exceedingly difficult and perhaps impossible, since such styles are in a certain way infinite--and delightful in different and various ways, on account of which a variety of compositional practices arises. Thus they are omitted from this account.

---

different from these to be found; to write them down would be exceedingly difficult and perhaps impossible, because these different styles of singing are in a certain way infinite--and they are delightful in different and various ways, on account of which a variety of compositional practices arises. Our intellect cannot grasp the infinite, since it is not of infinite but of finite capacity (otherwise it would be equal to the divine intellect, something not to be alleged). Thus, styles of this sort are omitted from this account; nor could they even be written down, because they are infinite.

5

1. Hiis visis, aliquid de ficta musica, que huic arti neccessaria est, est pertractandum, unde ficta musica est vocum fictio sive vocum positio in loco ubi esse non videntur, sicut ponere mi ubi non est mi, et fa ubi non est fa, et sic ultra, de qua ficta musica est primo sciendum

---

2-72.2 *Huc pertinet emendatio quae in L invenitur:* unde ficta musica est vocum fictio sive vocum positio in aliquo loco manus musicalis ubi nullo modo reperiuntur, sicut ponere mi ubi non est mi, et fa ubi non est fa, et sic de aliis vocibus. De ista ergo ficta musica notande sunt

---

1 *Tit.*: Tractatus tercius, De ficta musica, Capitulum primum *fort. m. sec.* E | *post* Hiis ergo *del.* C | ficta]fita V || 2 arti *om.* B | ficta]fita V || 3 vocum positio]positio V || 5 ficta]fita V ||

5

1. Now that these things have been examined, we must study something of musica ficta, which is necessary to this art.[1] Musica ficta is the feigning of syllables or the placement of syllables in a location where they do not seem to be--to apply mi where there is no mi and fa where there is no fa, and so forth.[2] Concerning musica

---

2-72.2: Musica ficta is the feigning of syllables or the placement of syllables in any location on the musical hand where they are in no way to be found--to apply mi where there is no mi and fa where there is no fa, and thus for the other syllables. Concerning musica ficta,

---

[1]Treatises that call musica ficta necessary include Philippe de Vitry, *Ars nova* 14.7-11, 18-19 (*Philippi de Vitriaco ars nova*, ed. Gilbert Reaney, André Gilles, and Jean Maillard, Corpus scriptorum de musica, no. 8 [N.p.: American Institute of Musicology, 1964], pp. 22-23); Petrus dictus Palma ociosa, *Compendium* (Wolf ed., p. 513); *Volentibus introduci*, Version AC 1.1 (CS, 3:26a); Ugolino, *Declaratio* 2.34.5, 10 (Seay ed., 2:44-45).

[2]Theorists frequently define musica ficta (or musica falsa) as the fashioning of semitones (or the application of accidentals) where they do not normally occur: "Sometimes by means of musica falsa we make a semitone where there should not be one (aliquando per falsam musicam facimus semitonium ubi non debet esse)" (Philippe de Vitry, *Ars nova* 14.2 [Reaney, Gilles, and Maillard ed., p. 22]); "Musica falsa is that which cannot be found in the gamut according to the art of plain chant. . . . Musica falsa is properly defined as the placement of round b or square ♮ where they are not [normally] used (Falsa musica est quae non potest inveniri in Gamma manus secundum artem plani cantus. . . . Falsa musica dicitur proprie, quando locabitur b molle vel ♮ quadratum in locis non usitatis)"

quod ipsa nunquam ponenda est nisi loco neccessitatis, eo quod in arte nichil est ponendum sine neccessitate.

2. Item sciendum quod ficta musica inventa est solum propter consonantiam aliquam colorandam, que consonantia aliter colorari non posset quam per fictam musicam. Et ex istis duobus notabilibus apparere potest quomodo quasi omnes cantuum compositores circa hanc fictam musicam sepissime errant, quoniam ipsa multotiens utuntur in loco ubi

---

hee regule, quarum prima est hec, quod ficta musica nunquam ponenda est nisi loco neccessitatis, eo quod in arte nichil est ponendum, et maxime fictio, sine neccessitate. 3 *Huc pertinet emendatio quae in L invenitur:* Secunda regula est hec, quod ficta musica . . . 5-8 *Huc pertinet emendatio quae in L invenitur:* Et ex istis duabus regulis apparet manifeste quomodo quasi omnes cantuum compositores circa hanc fictam musicam sepissime errant in suos cantus figurando, . . .

---

2 nichil ponendum est in arte E || 3 *post* sciendum: est E | ficta]fita V || 4 aliquam colorandam, que consonantia *om.* V || 5 posset]poterat L | fictam]fitam V || 6 quasi *in marg.* E || 8 utuntur multotiens C ||

ficta, it is necessary to know first of all that it is never to be applied except where necessary,[3] because in art nothing is to be applied without necessity.

2. It must be known, too, that musica ficta was invented exclusively for the sake of coloring some consonance that could not be colored except by musica ficta.[4] From these two points it can become evident that almost all composers of song very often err with respect to musica ficta, since they very frequently use it were there is

---

these rules must be noted, the first of which is this: that musica ficta is never to be applied except where necessary, because in art nothing--least of all a feigning--is to be applied without necessity. 3: The second rule is this: that musica ficta . . . 5-8: From these two rules it appears plainly that almost all composers of song very often err with respect to musica ficta in notating their melodies, . . .

(Petrus dictus Palma ociosa, *Compendium* [Wolf ed., pp. 513, 515]); "Musica ficta occurs when we make a whole tone a semitone or, conversely, a semitone a whole tone (Est ficta musica quando de tono facimus semitonium, et e converso de semitonio tonum)" (*Volentibus introduci*, Version AC 2.1 [CS, 3:26a]); "Musica ficta is the placement--necessary for the perfecting of a consonance--where it of itself does not lie (Musica ficta est alicuius vocis in loco ubi per se non est ad consonantiae perfectionem necessaria positio)" (Ugolino, *Declaratio* 2.34.3-4 [Seay ed., 2:44-45); "Musica ficta is melody brought forth outside the regular tradition of the [Guidonian] hand (Ficta musica est cantus praeter regularem manus traditionem aeditus)" (Tinctoris, *Dictionary of Musical Terms*, pp. 32-33, as corrected by Edward E. Lowinsky, "Renaissance Writings on Music Theory [1964]," *Renaissance News* 18 [1965]:361-62; cf. the Introduction of the present edition, p. 12).

[3]On the use of musica ficta, cf. Ugolino, *Declaratio* 2.34.12 (Seay ed., 2:45): "We do not use musica ficta at all without cogent necessity (musica ficta nisi necessitate cogente penitus non utamur)."

[4]Cf. Ugolino, *Declaratio* 2.34.80 (Seay ed., 2:53): "Musica ficta was invented by necessity in a melody, or for its decoration and beauty (Ficta musica ad cantus necessitatem eiusque ornatum atque decorem inventa est)."

non est neccessitas, sicut verbi gratia quando ad clavem de natura ponunt b rotundum sive molle, scilicet in Elami gravi, quia tunc illud b rotundum sive molle ponere possent ad clavem ♮ quadri sive duri, scilicet in bfa♮mi acuto, absque aliqua fiçta musica, et idem in opere proveniret, scilicet in eorum discantibus, sicut apparere potest cuilibet subtiliter consideranti.

3. Item sciendum quod signa huius ficte musice sunt duo, scilicet b rotundum sive molle et ♮ quadrum sive durum, que duo signa nobis demonstrant vocum fictionem in loco ubi tales voces esse non possunt, unde ubicumque ponitur b rotundum sive molle dicere debemus hanc vocem

---

1-7 *Huc pertinet emendatio quae in L invenitur:* . . . quando ad clavem de natura ponunt b rotundum sive molle, sic quod corpus ipsius b cadit in spacio Elami gravis, nam tunc illud b ponere possent ad clavem ♮ quadri sive duri, sic quod corpus ipsius b caderet in spacio bfa♮mi acuti absque aliqua ficta musica, et idem in opere proveniret, in tenore, contratenore, et suis discantibus. 8 *Huc pertinet emendatio quae in L invenitur:* Tercia regula est hec, quod signa . . . 10-76.2 *Huc pertinet emendatio quae in L invenitur:* . . . que duo signa nobis quandoque demonstrant vocum fictionem sive positionem in loco ubi ipse voces esse non possunt, unde ubicumque ponitur corpus b rotundi sive mollis, sive sit in linea sive in spacio,

---

2-3 scilicet . . . molle *om.* V ‖ 3 molle sive rotundum E | possunt V ‖ 4 bfa♮mi]bfabmi C ‖ 5 ficta]fita V ‖ 7 consideranti subtiliter C ‖ 9 molle]b molle V | ♮]b V ‖ 10 durum]duorum V | que duo signa]que signa E | fictionem *alt.* C ‖ 12 b rotundum sive molle]♮ quadrum sive durum C | debemus]demus V ‖

no necessity[5]--as for instance when they apply the round or soft b in a natural signature--as on low Elami,[6] because in that case they could apply the round or soft b to the signature representing square or hard ♮, high bfa♮mi,[7] without any musica ficta, and that same sign would result in the piece--in its discants--as can become evident to whoever considers the matter closely.

3. It must be known, too, that the signs of musica ficta are two, round or soft b and square or hard ♮. These two signs show us the feigning of syllables in a location where such syllables cannot be; wherever round or soft b is applied, we ought to sing the syllable fa, and wherever

---

1-7: . . . when they apply the round or soft b in a natural signature--so that the body of the b falls in the space of low Elami, for in that case they could apply the b to the signature representing square or hard ♮, so that the body of the b would fall in the space of high bfa♮mi without any musica ficta, and that same sign would result in the piece--in the tenor, the contratenor, and its discants. 8: The third rule is this: that the signs . . . 10-76.2: These two signs sometimes[8] show us the feigning of syllables or their placement in a location where these syllables cannot be; wherever the body of round or soft b is applied, whether on a line or in a space, we ought

---

[5]On Prosdocimo's criticism of composers who err in the use of musica ficta, see the Introduction, pp. 10-13.

[6]I.e., e. The round or soft b would make the e natural an e flat.

[7]I.e., b.

[8]In the original version, Prosdocimo says the signs indicate the feigning of syllables where such syllables cannot be. In the revision he adds the important qualification "sometimes (quandoque)": a round b attached to the b below middle c does not indicate a feigned syllable, for instance, because fa normally occurs there. Cf. Prosdocimo's *Tractatus musice speculative* (Baralli and Torri ed., p. 751): "These signs do not always indicate the feigning of music. Sometimes they do and sometimes they do not, as can clearly appear to whoever considers the matter carefully (Talia signa non semper denotant fictionem aliquam musice. Sed quandoque sic et quandoque non ut clare patere potest cuilibet bene consideranti)."

fa, et ubicumque ponitur ♮ quadrum sive || durum dicere debemus hanc vocem mi, sive tales voces ibidem sint sive non, cuius ratio est quia in hac dictione bfa♮mi, in qua ponitur utrumque istorum b, immediate ante fa ponitur b rotundum sive molle, et tali voci fa famulatur, immediate vero ante mi ponitur ♮ quadrum sive durum et tali voci mi famulatur, et ideo ad b rotundum sive molle dicimus fa, et ad ♮ quadrum sive durum dicimus mi. CS 19

4. Item sciendum quod hec duo signa sunt signa totaliter opposita, eo quod modo opposito totaliter operantur, quoniam si sit in ascensu b rotundum sive molle ascensum diminuit, et ♮ quadrum ipsum augmentat. Si vero sit in descensu fit e contrario, quoniam tunc b rotundum descensum augmentat et ♮ quadrum ipsum diminuit; et non addunt vel diminuunt ista duo signa nisi semitonium maius, quod semitonium est excessus quo maior combinatio ipsammet minorem excedit, ut supra dictum est.

---

ibi dicere debemus hanc vocem fa, et ubicumque ponitur corpus ♮ quadri sive duri, sive sit in linea sive in spacio, ibi dicere debemus hanc vocem mi, . . . 3-4 *Huc pertinet emendatio quae in L invenitur:* . . . in qua ponitur utrumque istorum b, scilicet rotundum et quadrum, . . . 7-8 *Huc pertinet emendatio quae in L invenitur:* . . . et ideo ad corpus b rotundi sive mollis dicimus hanc vocem fa, et ad corpus ♮ quadri sive duri dicimus hanc vocem mi. 9 *Huc pertinet emendatio quae in L invenitur:* Quarta regula est hec, quod hec duo signa . . .

---

1 fa]mi C | ♮]b V | ♮ quadrum sive durum]b rotundum sive molle C || 1-2 debemus dicere E || 2 mi]fa C || 3 bfa♮mi]bfabmi V | qua *om.* C || 7 mi *om.* C | famulatur mi E | ad]a V || 8 ad *om.* C | ♮]b V | sive durum *om.* E || 9 *post* sciendum: est E | signa(*sec.*)]sibi invicem L || 10 opposita]apposita V | eo quod]et L | operatur C || 11 sit]sic V || 12 ♮]b V | ♮ quadrum ipsum augmentat]♮ quadrum sive durum ipsum ascensum augmentat L | sit]sic V || 13 *post* fit equario *del.* C | b rotundum tunc C || 14 ipsum]ipsum descensum L || 15 semitonium maius]semitonium dyatonicum sive maius E || 15-16 quod semitonium est]quod est semitonium C quod semitonium maius est L || 16 excessus *legi non potest* V | ipsammet *legi non potest* V ||

square or hard ♮ is applied, we ought to sing the syllable mi,[9] whether or not these syllables are in those places. The reason for this is that in the expression bfa♮mi, in which both of these b's are applied, round or soft b is applied just before fa, and fa serves for this syllable; and square or hard ♮ is applied just before mi, and mi serves for this syllable, and thus at round or soft b we sing fa and at square or hard ♮ we sing mi.

4. It must be known, too, that these two signs are totally opposite signs, because they work in totally opposite ways. If round or soft b occurs in ascent it lessens the ascent; square ♮ augments it. In descent, on the contrary, the situation is reversed. Round b augments the descent and square ♮ diminishes it. The two signs do not augment or diminish intervals except by a major semitone, and this semitone is the amount by which a major interval exceeds the corresponding minor interval, as stated above.

---

to sing the syllable fa, and wherever the body of square or hard ♮ is applied, whether on a line or in a space, we ought to sing the syllable mi, . . . 3-4: . . . in which both of these b's (round and square) are applied, . . . 7-8: . . . and thus at the body of round or soft b we sing the syllable fa and at the body of square or hard ♮ we sing the syllable mi. 9: The fourth rule is this: that these two signs . . .

---

[9]It is a commonplace in medieval theory that round b indicates fa and square ♮ mi. Cf. Anonymous II, *Tractatus de discantu*, ed. Albert Seay, Critical Texts with Translation, no. 1 (Colorado Springs: Colorado College Music Press, 1978), p. 32; Marchetto, *Lucidarium* 8.1.8-10 (Herlinger ed.), where the rule is attributed to a Richardus Normandus; *Volentibus introduci*, Version AC 2.1 (CS, 3:26a); Ugolino, *Declaratio* 2.34.29-30 (Seay ed., 2:46).

5. Scias tamen quod quando hec signa ponuntur propter aliquam consonantiam colorandam, semper poni debent immediate ante notam que in voce propter talem consonantiam colorandam varianda est, sive talis nota sit in tenore sive in discantu, et sive ipsa sit in linea sive in spacio, cum quodlibet tale signum non deserviat nisi note immediate sequenti ipsum.

6. Item ultimo pro noticia collocationis istorum duorum signorum, scilicet b rotundi et ♮ quadri, est sciendum quod octavis, quintis, et hiis similibus ponenda sunt hec signa secundum quod oportet addere vel diminuere ad ipsas reducendum ad bonas consonantias, si prius forent dissonantes, eo quod tales combinationes in contrapuncto

---

1-2 *Huc pertinet emendatio quae in L invenitur:* Quinta regula est hec, quod quando aliquod horum duorum signorum ponitur propter aliquam consonantiam colorandam, semper poni debet . . . 4-5 *Huc pertinet emendatio quae in L invenitur:* . . . sive talis nota sit in tenore sive in contratenore sive in aliquo discantuum, . . . 6-7 *Huc pertinet emendatio quae in L invenitur:* . . . quodlibet tale signum non deserviat nisi note ipsum immediate sequenti, nisi b rotundum in principio alicuius cantus pro clavi poneretur, quoniam tunc ipsum b totum cantum denominat cantari debere per b rotundum sive molle, et ratio huius est quoniam nisi sic esset, multe voces per hec signa variarentur, que nullo modo essent variande, et sic variate quandoque dissonantiam facerent, vel tot de istis duobus signis nos in quolibet cantu cum alio consonantiam habere debente vel saltim in uno ipsorum oporteret ponere, quod, ut sic loquar, tot essent signa quot note, quod in hac arte malum esset, cum pluralitas sine neccessitate sit in qualibet arte dimittenda, quare et cetera. 8-11 *Huc pertinet emendatio quae in L invenitur:* Sexta et ultima regula pro noticia collocationis horum duorum signorum in contrapuncto, scilicet b rotundi et ♮ quadri, est hec, quod octavis, quintis, et sibi similibus ponenda sunt hec signa . . .

---

1 ponuntur *legi non potest* V || 2 debet C || 3-4 propter talem consonantiam colorandam in voce L || 5 sit ipsa L | in (*sec.*) *sup. lin.* B | *post* linea [[vel in spacio]] *del.* C || 6 note]*fort.* voce V || 8 ultimo *legi non potest* V || 9 signorum *legi non potest* V || 12 reducendum ipsas L | forent]fuissent L ||

5. You should know that when these signs are applied in order to color some consonance, they ought always to be applied just before the note whose syllable is to be changed in order to color the consonance, whether the note be in the tenor or the discant, and whether it be on a line or in a space, for any such sign serves only the note immediately following it.

6. Last, for understanding the placement of these two signs, round b and square ♮, it must be known that these signs are to be applied to octaves, fifths, and similar intervals as it is necessary to enlarge or diminish them in order to make them good consonances if they earlier were dissonant, because such intervals ought always to

---

1-2: The fifth rule is this: that when either of these two signs is applied in order to color some consonance, it ought always to be applied . . . 4-5: . . . whether the note be in the tenor or in the contratenor or in one of the discants, . . . 6-7: . . . any such sign serves only the note immediately following it (unless the round b is applied at the beginning of some melody as a signature, because in that case the b signifies that the whole melody ought to be sung with round or soft b). The reason for this is, if it were not so, many syllables would be altered by this sign that should not be altered in any way, and, thus altered, would sometimes create dissonance. Or we would be obliged to apply so many of these two signs in every melody that had to be consonant with another (or at least in one of the melodies) that, so to speak, there would be as many signs as notes, which would be bad in this art, since multiplicity without necessity is to be rejected in any art. More could be said about this. 8-11: The sixth and last rule, for understanding the placement of these two signs, round b and square ♮, in counterpoint, is this: that these signs are to be applied to octaves, fifths, and similar intervals . . .

semper maiores sive consonantes esse debent. Sed in vocum combinationibus imperfecte consonantibus, sicut sunt tercia, sexta, decima, et huiusmodi, ponenda sunt etiam hec signa secundum quod oportet addere vel diminuere in || ipsas CS 19 reducendo ad maioritatem vel minoritatem opportunas, eo quod tales combinationes in contrapuncto esse debent aliquando maiores et aliquando minores; et si hanc diversitatem scire cupis, quando, scilicet, ipse debent esse maiores et quando minores, considerare debes locum ad quem immediate accedere debes post tuum recessum a tali consonantia imperfecta, et tunc videre debes an locus a quo recedis magis distet a loco ad quem immediate accedere intendis, faciendo talem consonantiam imperfectam maiorem an in faciendo

---

4 *post* ipsas ca *del.* C || 4-5 reducendo ipsas L || 6-7 aliquando maiores et aliquando minores esse debent E || 8 debent ipse L || 11 debes]intendis L || 12 immediate]mediate V | accedere *om.* V || 13 imperfectam maiorem]imperfectam et maiorem V ||

be major or consonant in counterpoint. But these signs are to be applied to imperfectly consonant intervals--the third, the sixth, the tenth, and the like--as is necessary to enlarge or diminish them to give them major or minor inflections as appropriate, because such intervals ought sometimes to be major and sometimes minor in counterpoint;[10] and if you wish to know the difference--when they should be major and when minor--you should consider the location to which you must move immediately after leaving the imperfect consonance; then you must see whether the location you leave is more distant from that location which you intend immediately to reach, making the imperfect consonance

---

[10]Theorists frequently recommend the use of musica ficta to make fifths, octaves, and the like perfect and to make imperfect consonances lie as close as possible to their perfectly consonant destinations. Perhaps the earliest statement of the underlying principles--*causa necessitatis* and *causa pulchritudinis*--appears in Anonymous II, who, however, applied the latter only to a monophonic repertoire (*Tractatus de discantu* [Seay ed., p. 32]): "Musica falsa was invented for two reasons, because of necessity and because of beauty in the song itself--because of necessity, since otherwise we could not have a fifth, a fourth, or an octave, as in the matters discussed in the chapter on proportions; because of beauty, as appears in the 'crowned songs' (Fuit autem inventa falsa musica propter duas causas, scilicet, causa necessitatis et causa pulchritudinis cantus per se. Causa necessitatis, quia non poteramus habere diapente, diatessaron, diapason, ut in locis visis in capitulo de proportionibus. Causa pulchritudinis, ut patet in cantilenis [ms.: cantinellis] coronatis)." The "crowned songs," discussed by Johannes de Grocheio, *De musica* 112 (*Die Quellenhandschriften zum Musiktraktat des Johannes de Grocheio*, ed. Ernst Rohloff [Leipzig: VEB Deutscher Verlag für Musik, 1972], pp. 130-31), are trouvère songs. According to Hendrik van der Werf, *The Chansons of the Troubadours and Trouvères: A Study of Their Melodies and Their Relation to the Poems* (Utrecht: Oosthoek, 1972), p. 154, it is not clear whether the term "refers exclusively to prize-winning songs, to trouvère chansons in general, or to a specific category of trouvère chansons." Petrus dictus Palma ociosa, *Compendium* (Wolf ed., pp. 514-15), shows alteration of both perfect and imperfect consonances in his examples, and Ugolino, *Declaratio* 2.34.33-34 (Seay ed., 2:46-47), discusses both types explicitly.

ipsam minorem, quoniam illam semper sumere debes que minus distat a loco ad quem immediate accedere intendis, sive illa sit maior sive minor, et debes tunc facere ipsam per signa superius posita, de maiori minorem vel e contra, scilicet de minori maiorem, secundum quod oportet, cuius ratio non est alia quam dulcior armonia. Sed quare hec dulcior armonia ex hoc proveniat potest talis assignari ratio satis persuasiva, quoniam si de ratione imperfecti sit sui appetere perfectionem, quod aliter esse non potest quam per approximationem sui ad rem perfectam. Hinc est quod quanto consonantia imperfecta magis appropinquat perfecte ad quam accedere intendit, tanto perfectior effici-

---

8-9 *Huc pertinet emendatio quae in L invenitur:* . . . quoniam si de ratione imperfecti vel minus perfecti sit sui appetere perfectionem vel perfectius effici, quod aliter esse non potest . . . 11-12 *Huc pertinet emendatio quae in L invenitur:* . . . quanto consonantia imperfecta magis appropinquat alteri consonantie ad quam immediate accedere intendit, . . .

---

1 minus]unius C || 2 quem]quam V || 3 tunc *om.* V | ipsam]ipsa V || 6 non est alia]est et non alia E | dulcior *fort. ex* dulcis *alt.* E || 7 *post* armonia unde *del.* C || 10 per]propter BE || 12 perfectior]perficior C ||

major or making it minor: for you should always choose that form, whether major or minor, that is less distant from that location which you intend immediately to reach,[11] and you should, by means of the signs posited above, make a major interval minor or, contrariwise, a minor one major as appropriate. There is no other reason for this than a sweeter-sounding harmony. Why the sweeter-sounding harmony results from this can be ascribed to the sufficiently persuasive reason that the property of the imperfect thing is to seek the perfect, which it cannot do except through approximating itself to the perfect. This is because the closer the imperfect consonance approaches the perfect one it intends to reach, the more perfect

---

8-9: . . . that the property of the imperfect or less perfect thing is to seek the perfect or to become more perfect, which it cannot do . . . 11-12: . . . the closer the imperfect consonance approaches the other consonance[12] it intends immediately to reach, . . .

---

[11]Among theorists who call for the closest approach of an imperfect consonance to a perfect one are Marchetto, *Lucidarium* 5.6.2-7 (Herlinger ed.); Petrus dictus Palma ociosa, *Compendium* (Wolf ed., pp. 513-15); *Quilibet affectans* (CS, 3:59b-60a); Goscalcus, *Tractatus de contrapuncto* (Ellsworth ed., 1:31); Ugolino, *Declaratio* 2.6.7, 9 (Seay ed., 2:13); Ramos, *Musica practica* 2.1.1 (Wolf ed., p. 65); Burzio, *Florum libellus* 2.2.15 (Massera ed., p. 118); Gaffurio, *Practica musicae* 3.3.

[12]In the revision, Prosdocimo alters the clause, "the closer the imperfect consonance approaches the perfect one it intends to reach, the more perfect it becomes" by substituting "other consonance" for "perfect one." He thus becomes probably the first theorist to advocate chromatic alteration of an imperfect consonance that moves to another imperfect one. See the Introduction, p. 13.

tur, et inde dulcior armonia causatur. Et ut melius supradicta intelligantur, pono hoc exemplum:

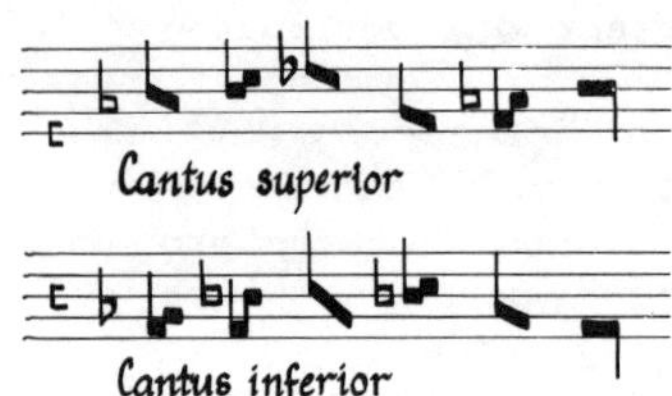

1-2 *Huc pertinet emendatio quae in L invenitur:* Et ut melius hec iam supradicta de collocatione horum duorum signorum intelligantur, pono hoc exemplum:

---

1 et inde]atque inde L | dulcior *bis* (*primum del.*) E | causatur]producitur L || *transcriptio exempli in semibrevibus in marg.* B | *cantus inferior sine tit.* V ||

it becomes, and the sweeter the resulting harmony.[13] And so that what has been said above may be the better understood, I present this example:

1-2: And so that what has already been said above about the placement of these two signs may be the better understood, I present this example:

---

[13]The explanation Prosdocimo gives for the "closest approach" principle is paraphrased from Marchetto, *Lucidarium* 5.6.5-7 (Herlinger ed.): "The reason is that a dissonance is something imperfect; it requires something perfect by means of which it can be perfected. The consonance is its perfection. The less distant the dissonance lies from the consonance the less distant it is from its perfection and the more it is assimilated to it, and thus the more agreeable it is to the ear, as if it partook more of the nature of the consonance (Hoc ideo est, eo quod dissonantia sit quoddam imperfectum, requirens perfectum, quo perfici possit. Consonantia autem est perfectio ipsius. Quanto enim dissonantia minus distat a consonantia, tanto minus distat a sua perfectione et magis assimilatur eidem, et ideo magis amicabilis est auditui, tamquam plus habens de natura consonantie)." (For Marchetto, "consonance" means perfect consonance; "dissonance" includes the category of imperfect consonance.) Cf. also Ugolino, *Declaratio* 2.34.34 (Seay ed., 2:47): "The cause of the nearer thing's acquiring perfection is that every imperfect consonance or dissonance, as something imperfect, strives for its perfection, strives to be made perfect. The closer it lies to perfection, the sooner it is made perfect (Causa vero propinquioris acquirendae perfectionis est quia cum

‖ Unde si hec signa in hoc exemplo posita bene consideras, primum ♮ quadrum in cantu superiori positum facit illam sextam minorem esse maiorem, eo quod in sua maioritate minus distat a loco ad quem accedere intendit, scilicet ab octava maiori immediate sequenti, quam in sua minoritate; b vero molle sive rotundum in cantu superiori repertum facit illam sextam maiorem esse minorem, eo quod in sua minoritate minus distat a loco ad quem accedere intendit, scilicet ab octava maiori immediate sequenti, quam in sua maioritate; et per simile ponitur primum ♮ quadrum in cantu inferiori et propter eandem causam, quoniam talis sexta in sua minoritate minus distat a loco ad quem immediate accedere intendit, scilicet ab alia sexta immediate sequenti, quam in sua maioritate; ♮ vero quadrum secundum in cantu superiori repertum positum est propter eandem causam propter quam positum est et primum ipsius cantus superioris; sed ♮ quadrum secundum in cantu inferiori positum facit illam terciam maiorem esse minorem, eo quod in sua minoritate minus distat a loco ad quem accedere intendit, scilicet ab unisono immediate sequenti, quam in sua maioritate, et hec omnia comprehendere poterit quilibet boni ingenii si ipsa subtiliter speculabitur. CS 19

---

4 *Huc pertinet emendatio quae in L invenitur:* . . . a loco ad quem immediate accedere intendit, . . . 19-20 *Huc pertinet emendatio quae in L invenitur:* . . . a loco ad quem immediate accedere intendit, . . . 20-22 *Huc pertinet emendatio quae in L invenitur:* . . . quam in sua maioritate, que omnia comprehendere poterit quilibet boni ingenii in hac arte aliquantulum intelligens ad supradicta subtiliter inspiciendo; b vero rotundum in cantu inferiori positum totum cantum denominat per b molle sive rotundum cantari debere et pro clavi ibi ponitur.

Patet ergo ex hiis que dicta sunt de istis signis manifeste error modernorum qui loco ♮ quadri ponunt talem crucem, ♯, sive talem, ✗, secundum moderniores, et denominant hec sua signa hoc nomine, dyesis, vel falsa musica,

---

1 si]per C | consideres V ‖ 3 sextam *om.* C ‖ 5-9 quam in sua . . . immediate sequenti *om.* C ‖ 6-10 b vero molle . . . quam in sua maioritate *om.* L ‖ 8 minus *om.* V | quem *in marg.* V ‖ 10 maioritate *ex* minoritate *alt.* E | ♮ quadrum primum C ‖ 11 et]repertum et etiam L | eadem V ‖ 12 minus]unius C | quem]*fort.* quam V ‖ 16 est *om.* V ‖ 17 ♮ *om.* C ‖ 22 *post* qui (*ex* quilibet) liq *del.* C ‖

If you carefully consider the signs placed in this example, you will see that the first square ♮ placed in the upper melody makes that minor sixth major, because in its major inflection it is less distant from the location it intends to reach--the major octave immediately following--than in its minor inflection. The soft or round b found in the upper melody makes that major sixth minor, because in its minor inflection it is less distant from the location it intends to reach--the major octave immediately following--than in its major inflection. Similarly, the first square ♮ in the lower melody is placed there for the same reason. This sixth in its minor inflection is less distant from the location it intends to reach immediately--the other sixth immediately following--than in its major inflection. The second square ♮ found in the upper melody is placed there for the same reason as the first in that upper melody; the second square ♮ placed in the lower melody makes that major third minor, because in its minor inflection it is less distant from the location it intends to reach--the unison immediately following--than in its major inflection. Anyone of sound intellect will be able to understand all these things if he will examine them closely.

4: . . . from the location it intends immediately to reach . . . 19-20: . . . from the location it intends immediately to reach . . . 20-22: . . . than in its major inflection. Anyone of sound intellect who is knowledgeable in this art to some degree will be able to understand all these things by considering them closely. The round b placed in the lower melody indicates that the entire melody should be sung with soft or round b; it is placed there as a signature.

From what has been said of these signs, the error of those modern writers lies open who in place of square ♮ apply this cross ♯, or, according to the more modern ones, this, 𝄪, and call these signs of theirs by the name diesis or falsa musica, following the bad doctrine of

---

omnis consonantia imperfecta sive dissonantia tamquam imperfectum quoddam suam appetat perfectionem et perfici, et tanto citius perficiatur, quanto sit illi propinquior perfectioni)." Sachs called attention to the relationship of Marchetto, Prosdocimo, and Ugolino, *Contrapunctus*, p. 107.

doctrinam malam Marcheti paduani supradicti in sequendo. Fuit ergo predictus Marchetus principium huius erroris. In cantu namque superiori pro exemplo supraposito dixisset

the aforementioned Marchetto of Padua.[14] The aforesaid Marchetto was the source of this error. Regarding the upper melody of the example given above, Marchetto would

---

[14]Marchetto was, as Prosdocimo declares, the first to introduce a third chromatic sign: "The signs that indicate we are to make a permutation are three, the square ♮, the round b, and another sign commonly called falsa musica (Signa autem quibus nobis innuitur permutationem facere sunt tria, scilicet ♮ quadrum, b rotundum, et aliud signum, quod a vulgo falsa musica nominatur)" (*Lucidarium* 8.1.4 [Herlinger ed.]). The most authoritative source for Marchetto's treatises has ♯ (as opposed to the signs b and ♮), and this agrees with his instructions for drawing it: "Let this sign be made with a certain property exceeding [that of] the square ♮, thus, ♯. It suffices to draw more projecting end lines for it than for the square ♮, especially a line that projects upward on the right (Fiat tale signum cum quadam proprietate supra ♮ quadrum, ut hic ♯. Sufficit enim ultimiores protractiones facere in ipso quam in ♮ quadro. Et maxime in tali signo in sursum et a parte dextra)" (*Pomerium* 17.15-17 (*Marcheti de Padua pomerium*, ed. Giuseppe Vecchi, Corpus scriptorum de musica, no. 6 (Rome: American Institute of Musicology, 1961), p. 73, with accidentals taken from the manuscript Milan, Biblioteca Ambrosiana, D.5. inferiore]).

Marchetto, however, disapproves of the confusion of the two signs no less than does Prosdocimo: "There are some who write the square ♮ and the third sign . . . in the same manner, totally ignoring their true and different properties. The true property of the square ♮ is to divide the whole tone into an enharmonic semitone and a diatonic one or vice versa . . . ; the true property of the other sign is to divide the tone into a chromatic semitone and a diesis, or to divide the enharmonic semitone in half, in order to reach consonances after dissonances (Sunt enim nonnulli qui ipsum ♮ et tercium signum . . . eodem modo figurant, propriam proprietatem et diversam eorum penitus ignorantes; nam propria proprietas ♮ est semper dividere tonum per enarmonicum et diatonicum semitonia, vel e converso . . . ; alterius signi propria proprietas est tonum dividere per cromaticum et diesim et semitonium enarmonicum per medietatem, pro quibusdam . . . consonantiis post dissonantias assumendis)" (*Lucidarium* 8.1.17-20

---

dictus Marchetus quod ascensus qui est ab e acuto ad f acutum fuisset semitonium cromaticum quatuor dyesium, ita quod

---

have said that the ascending interval from high e to high f[15] would have been a chromatic semitone of four dieses,

---

[Herlinger ed.]). The difference between the two signs is that the square ♮ is used in perfect consonances, the *falsa musica* sign in imperfect consonances that proceed to perfect ones (see *Lucidarium* 2.6-8, and Jan W. Herlinger, "Marchetto's Division of the Whole Tone," *Journal of the American Musicological Society* 34 [1981]:193-216):

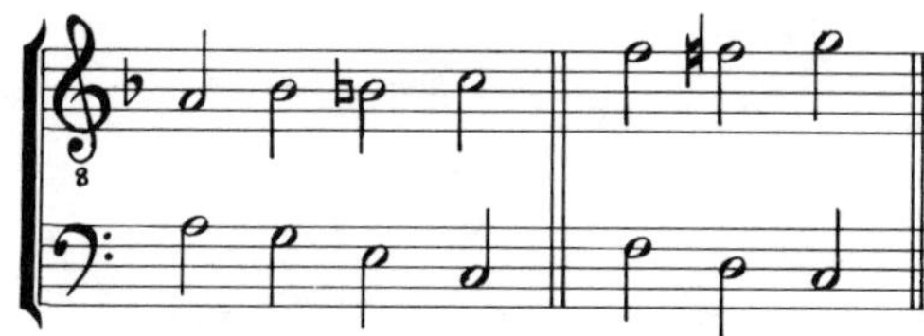

In Marchetto's system, the interval between f and f#, marked by the *falsa musica* sign, is four dieses, that between b♭ and b♮, marked with the square ♮, three dieses.

Marchetto regards the distinction between the signs as valid and condemns those who do not observe it. Whether the distinction was ever widely observed is not known. F. Alberto Gallo has discovered one manuscript fragment in Venice that does distinguish the signs; see his "Da un codice italiano di motetti del primo Trecento," *Quadrivium* 9 (1968):25-35. Prosdocimo, on the other hand, objects specifically to the use of either of the two signs in places where the square ♮ is appropriate. He shows us how Marchetto's ♯ had evolved over a hundred years and testifies that the name of the sign had changed from "falsa musica" to "diesis."

The present emendation incorporates much material from Prosdocimo's *Tractatus musice speculative* (Baralli and Torri ed., pp. 750-51).

[15]I.e., e' to f'. This interval, of course, does not occur in the example; Prosdocimo refers to it in the abstract.

Prosdocimo misunderstands Marchetto's system when he says that Marchetto would have called the interval

---

ad complementum toni non defecisset nisi una dyesis, et ita ad reducendum primam sextam et etiam secundam minores ad earum maioritatem, secundum ipsum, non deficit eis

---

so that only one diesis would be lacking to complete the whole tone, and thus--according to him--to make the first minor sixth and the second one major nothing would be

---

from e to f a chromatic semitone of four dieses and that Marchetto's chromatic sign would have added another diesis. For Marchetto, the interval between e and f is a minor or enharmonic semitone of two dieses, the interval between f and f marked with the *falsa musica* sign the chromatic semitone, or *chroma*, of four dieses (*Lucidarium* 2.7.2, 2.8.2-4 [Herlinger ed.]):

> The minor, or enharmonic, semitone is that which contains two dieses; we use it in plain chant. . . . The chromatic semitone is that which includes four of the five dieses of the whole tone, and, as said earlier, it completes a whole tone when a diesis is added to it. It results when some whole tone is divided in two so as to color some dissonance such as a third, a sixth, or a tenth striving toward some consonance. The first part of a tone thus divisible will be larger if the melody ascends, and is called a *chroma*; the part that remains is a diesis, as here: . . . (Semitonium minus seu enarmonicum est quod continet duas dyeses, quo quidem utimur in plano cantu. . . . Cromaticum semitonium est illud quod de quinque dyesibus quas habet tonus quatuor comprehendit, et, ut predicitur, semper cum dyesi tonum perficit. Fit enim cum aliquis tonus bipartitur propter aliquam dissonantiam colorandam, puta terciam, sextam, sive decimam tendendo ad aliquam consonantiam, nam prima pars toni sic divisibilis, si per ascensum fiat, erit maior, que dicitur croma; pars que restat dyesis est, ut hic: . . .).

7. Sufficiant ergo ista de contrapuncto per musicorum minimum Prosdocimum de Beldemandis patavum, anno Domini 1412 in castro Montagnane paduani districtus breviter compilata. Deo gratias. Amen.

8. Explicit Contrapunctus Magistri Prosdocimi de Beldemandis paduani in castro Montagnane paduani districtus anno domini 1412 compilatus. Deo gratias. Amen.

---

nisi una dyesis, que postea sibi additur per illas suas cruces superius positas, quas, ut dixi, ponebat in loco in quo ♮ quadrum ponere debebat, et hac [*fort. ex* hoc *alt.*] de causa ipse et sui sequaces tales cruces hoc nomine, dyesis, nominaverunt, et hanc sententiam scribit ipse Marchetus in suo Lucidario, sed nec sibi nec suis sequacibus in hoc est fides adhibenda, quoniam, ut supradictum est, ibi ea scripsit que totaliter ignoravit.

Et ut adhuc maiorem noticiam de istis signis accipias, scire debes quod in huiusmodi combinationibus vocum variationibus quantum ad sui maioritatem vel minoritatem potes ponere signa supradicta, ita ad cantum superiorem sicut ad cantum inferiorem et e contra, unde si variatio aliqua in cantu superiori fiat per b rotundum, in cantu inferiori fiet per ♮ quadrum, et si in cantu superiori fiat variatio per ♮ quadrum in cantu inferiori fiet per b rotundum. Sed consulo tibi ut sis cautus in pondendo hec signa, quoniam ubi dulcius cadunt, ibi poni debent, unde si dulcius cadunt in tenore, ponantur in tenore, et si dulcius in discantu, ponantur in discantu. Si vero eque [*ms.*: equa] dulciter in discantu et tenore, potius ponantur in discantu quam in tenore, ne propter hoc oporteat etiam te ponere aliquod horum signorum ad contratenorum vel triplum vel quadruplum, si ibi reperiantur, ad que nichil horum signorum poneretur. Si signum opportunum sonans eque dulciter, ad discantum ponatur et non ad tenorem. Scire autem ubi hec signa dulcius cadunt auri tue dimitto, quia de hoc regula dari non potest, cum hec loca quodammodo infinita sint. 3-4 *Huc pertinet emendatio quae in L invenitur:* . . . taliter compilata ad gloriam omnipotentis Dei.

---

2 Beldemando L || 4 Deo gratias *om.* EL | Amen *om.* E || 5 Contrapunctus]tractatus E | Magistri *om.* CELV || 5-6 Prosdocimi de Beldemandis paduani *om.* E Prosdocimi de Beldemandis de Padua C Prosdocimi de Beldemando de Padua L || 6-7 in castro . . . Amen *om.* CE || 7 Deo gratias *om.* V ||

7. Then let these things suffice concerning counterpoint, briefly compiled by the least of musicians, the Paduan Prosdocimus de Beldemandis, in the year of the Lord 1412, in the fortified town of Montagnana in the Paduan jurisdiction. Thanks be to God. Amen.

8. Here ends the *Counterpoint* of the Paduan master Prosdocimus de Beldemandis, compiled in the fortified town of Montagnana in the Paduan jurisdiction, in the year of the Lord 1412. Thanks be to God. Amen.

---

lacking but a single diesis that would then be added by those crosses of his given above, which, as I said, he applied in the location where he should have applied a square ♮; this is why he and his followers called these crosses by the name diesis. Marchetto himself states this view in his *Lucidarium*. In this matter, neither he nor his followers are to be trusted, because, as said above, he wrote down things there of which he was totally ignorant.

And so that you might gain yet more understanding of these two signs, you should know that to vary these intervals with respect to their major and minor inflections you can apply these aforesaid signs to the upper voice as to the lower voice and contrariwise. If the alteration in the upper voice should be made with round b, it would be made in the lower voice with square ♮, and if the alteration should be made in the upper voice with square ♮, it would be made in the lower voice with round b. But I advise you to be circumspect in applying these signs, because they should be applied where they sound more agreeable. If they sound better in the tenor, they should be applied in the tenor; if they sound better in the discant, they should be applied in the discant. If they sound equally good in the discant and the tenor, they should be applied in the discant rather than the tenor, lest it be necessary to apply some one of these signs in the contratenor, the triplum, or the quadruplum (if they should be found there), to which none of these signs should be applied. If the appropriate sign sounds equally good, it should be applied to the discant and not the tenor. Knowing where the signs sound better I leave to your ear, because on this, no rule can be given, for the situations are in a certain way infinite. 3-4: . . . thus compiled for the glory of the omnipotent God.

APPENDIX

PROSDOCIMO AND UGOLINO

The following topics are treated similarly by Prosdocimo and by Ugolino of Orvieto (*Ugolini Urbevetanis declaratio musicae disciplinae*, 3 vols., ed. Albert Seay, Corpus scriptorum de musica, no. 7 [Rome: American Institute of Musicology, 1959-1962] [page numbers refer to vol. 2]):

Topic	Prosdocimo, *Contrapunctus*	Ugolino, *Declaratio* 2
Counterpoint in the ordinary or loose sense vs. that in the proper or strict sense	2.1 (pp. 28-30)	2.2, 4-6 (p. 4)
Counterpoint presupposes plain chant practice	2.3 (p. 32)	4.2 (p. 8)
Six syllables	3.1 (p. 34)	7.3 (p. 15)
Unison requires two notes in same location and with same syllable	3.2 (pp. 34-36)	4.4 (p. 8)
Consonance and dissonance	3.3 (pp. 38-40)	3.18-19, 21 (p. 6)
Perfect and imperfect consonance	3.4 (p. 42)	3.37-39 (p. 7) 4.6 (pp. 8-9)
Major and minor inflections of intervals	3.5 (pp. 44-48)	5.2-3, 7 (p. 10)
Major inflection exceeds minor by a major semitone	3.8 (p. 54)	5.26-29 (pp. 11-12)
Discords excluded from counterpoint	4.2 (p. 58)	3.36 (p. 7)
Counterpoint ends with perfect concord	4.3 (pp. 58-60)	6.3-4 (p. 12)

Parallel perfect concords prohibited	4.4 (pp. 60-62)	25.15 (p. 31)
Perfect concords required from time to time	4.5 (p. 62)	25.19 (p. 31)
Mi contra fa prohibited in perfect concords	4.6 (pp. 62-64)	25.22-23 (p. 31)
Parallel imperfect concords allowed, provided perfect ones appear from time to time; alternation of perfect concords with intermediate imperfect ones	4.7 (pp. 64-68)	25.17-18, 20-21 (p. 31)
Musica ficta necessary; defined as placement of syllables in unaccustomed locations; not to be used except where necessary	5.1 (pp. 70-72)	34.3-4, 5, 10, 12 (pp. 44-45)
Musica ficta invented for coloring of concords	5.2 (pp. 72-74)	34.61-62 (p. 51)
Round b and square ♮	5.3 (pp. 74-76)	34.29-30 (p. 46)
Musica ficta used to perfect fifths and octaves, to alter imperfect concords	5.6 (pp. 78-80)	34.33-34 (pp. 46-47)
Imperfect concords to lie as close as possible to their perfect destinations	5.6 (pp. 80-82)	6.7, 9 (p. 13)
Beauty arises from closest approach of imperfect concords to perfect ones	5.6 (pp. 82-84)	34.34 (p. 47)

INDEX VERBORUM

accedere, 34.2; 80.10, 12; 82.2, 12; 86.4, 8, 13, 19
accessus, 66.6
accipi, 32.5, 6
acutus, 74.4
addere, 26.2; 52.19; 54.7; 76.14; 78.11; 80.4
admiratio, 32.12
admoveri, 60.2
agere, 60.14
agregatio, 34.4
alius, 28.4, 13; 32.14; 40.2; 50.7; 52.1; 82.6; 86.13
alter, 62.2, 5
ambo, 32.3, 36.11
amicabilis, 60.2
amoveri, 60.8
anima, 60.6
antiquus, 40.4; 46.7
apparere, 36.16, 72.6, 74.6
appetere, 82.9
appropinquare, 82.11
approximatio, 82.10
armonia, 58.7; 60.1, 2, 5, 7; 62.11 (bis); 66.1; 82.6, 7; 84.1
ars, 26.6; 32.9 (bis), 14, 15; 34.8; 58.8; 70.2; 72.2
ascendere, 60.10, 64.5
ascensus, 76.11 (bis)
asserere, 26.4
assignari, 82.7
assimilari, 36.1
auctor, 44.12; 46.7
auditor, 60.1, 4, 6
augmentare, 76.12, 14
auris, 34.3; 38.3, 7; 42.5, 9
b, 76.4; b rotundum, 74.2, 3, 9, 12; 76.5, 7, 11, 13; 78.9; 86.6
♮ quadrum, 74.4, 9; 76.1, 6, 8, 12, 14; 78.9; 86.2, 10, 14, 17
bfa♮mi, 36.15; 74.4; 76.3
binarius, 50.6, 11
bonus, 38.3; 42.8; 62.6; 78.12; 86.22

cadere, 66.3, 4, 5, 6
cantare, 62.1, 10; 66.9; 68.1; cantari, 28.4, 6; 30.5; 62.4
cantus, 28.1 (bis), 10, 14; 30.8; 34.11; 44.6; 58.9; 60.9; 64.5, 8; 72.7; 86.2, 6, 11, 15, 16, 17; cantus planus, 32.10
castrum, 94.3, 6
causa, 34.14; 86.11, 16
causari, 84.1
clavis, 74.1, 4
collocatio, 78.8
colorare, 72.4; 78.2, 4; colorari, 72.5
combinatio, 38.1, 2; 40.2; 42.1; 44.15; 46.1, 10; 48.2; 50.4; 52.18 (bis); 54.1, 3, 4, 5-6, 9; 58.1, 12; 60.11; 62.9, 13; 64.3-4, 6, 9; 66.8; 76.16; 78.13; 80.6; combinatio vocum, 34.1-2, 2, 7; 48.4; 50.2-3; 52.2, 5, 6, 9, 13, 15; 60.14; 62.8, 15; 80.1-2
compilari, 94.4, 7
componere, 68.4
compositor, 72.7
comprehendere, 50.2; 86.21
comunis, 52.4
concordans, 38.2; 50.3; 52.2, 5; 60.12, 14; 62.8; 64.7
concordantia, 62.2-3, 6
considerare, 74.7; 80.9; 86.1
consistere, 44.13; 46.8; 50.4
consonans, 38.2; 42.1; 44.15; 62.9, 14; 64.1, 4; 66.1; 80.1, 2
consonantia, 34.3; 38.3; 40.3, 5; 42.5, 8; 44.1-2, 11; 46.6; 60.3, 6, 7; 66.2, 7; 72.4 (bis); 78.2, 3, 12; 80.10, 13; 82.11
constituere, 64.1
contentus, 56.4-5
continere, 44.9, 14; 46.2, 3, 5, 9; 48.1; 52.7-8, 8, 11, 12, 14, 17
contrapositio, 28.16; 30.1 (bis), 3
contrapunctare, 60.10; 62.7; 64.6
contrapunctus, 26.5; 28.6, 8, 11, 12, 15; 30.2, 2-3, 5; 32.1, 4, 5, 9; 36.11; 44.5; 58.1-2, 6, 11; 62.3; 78.13; 80.6; 94.1, 5
contrarium, 76.13
cupere, 80.8
cura, 44.7
dari, 62.2
decima, 34.14; 36.4; 38.5; 42.7; 66.6; 80.3
decima nona, 36.5
decima octava, 36.5
decima septima, 36.4
decima sexta, 36.3

declarari, 34.1
declaratio, 34.1
delectabilis, 60.5; 66.1; 68.3
delectatio, 60.8
demi, 50.5
demonstrare, 74.10
denominari, 50.4, 6, 10, 14, 18
descendere, 60.11; 64.5
descensus, 76.13 (bis)
deservire, 78.6
determinare, 26.5; 28.11, 15
dicere, 34.2, 7; 40.4; 44.12; 46.8; 74.12; 76.1, 7, 8; dici, 30.3; 32.4-5; 34.14 (bis); 36.12; 42.4, 8; 54.1; 64.2; 76.17
dictio, 76.3
dignus, 28.2
dilatari, 54.1
diminuere, 54.7; 76.12, 14, 15; 78.11; 80.4
dimitti, 60.4
discantus, 74.6; 78.5
discordans, 38.7; 46.1, 11; 48.2-3; 50.3; 52.2-3, 5-6; 64.2
discordantia, 58.3
discretus, 50.1
dissonans, 38.6; 40.2; 78.13
dissonantia, 34.3; 38.7; 40.3; 44.2, 3, 5; 58.7, 10
dissonare, 40.1
distantia, 54.1
distare, 80.12; 82.2; 86.4, 8, 12, 19
districtus, 94.3, 6
diversitas, 68.4; 80.7
diversus, 60.13; 62.2, 5; 64.8; 68.3
dulcis, 60.2, 6; 66.9; 68.1; 82.6, 7; 84.1
dulcor, 60.5
duo, 28.1; 34.3; 36.14; 44.8, 14 (bis); 46.4, 5; 50.12, 17, 21; 52.1, 11, 14; 66.2; 72.6; 74.9, 10; 76.9, 15; 78.9
duodecima, 36.1, 6; 38.5; 42.4; 52.13, 15; 66.5
duplex, 32.2, 7
duplus, 46.8
duritia, 60.6
durus, 62.10; 74.4, 10; 76.1, 6, 8
effieri, 82.12-83.1
Elami, 74.2
elongari, 36.10
equivalens, 38.4, 8; 40.1; 42.3, 6-7; 58.5, 14; 60.13
errare, 72.8
excedere, 54.4; 76.17
excessus, 76.16

exemplum, 84.2; 86.1
existere, 36.18; 44.7; 58.8; 62.12
fa, 34.5; 36.15; 62.15; 70.4, 5; 76.1, 4, 5, 8
facere, 36.11; 44.3; 80.12, 13; 82.3; 86.2, 7, 18; fieri, 66.6, 9
famulari, 76.5, 7
ficta musica, 70.1, 2, 5; 72.7; 74.5, 8
fictio, 70.3; 74.10
finalis, 60.7
finiri, 58.12
finis, 58.8; 62.12
fractibilis, 30.8; 44.6; 58.9
fundamentum, 30.6
fundari, 32.6
gaudium, 60.8
grates, 26.3
gratia, 66.3; 74.1; 94.4, 7
gravis, 74.3
habere, 26.3; 28.4, 6, 12, 15; 30.5; 50.8, 12, 17, 21; 60.1; 64.9; haberi, 30.7 (bis), 32.11
huiusmodi, 30.5; 32.1; 38.9; 42.4, 7; 80.3
humanus, 38.3, 8; 42.5, 9
immediatus, 52.19; 66.3
imperfectus, 42.2, 6, 8, 9-10; 66.3, 7, 8; 80.10-11, 13; 82.8, 11
inchoari, 34.12
incipi, 34.11; 58.12
ineptitudo, 64.8-9
inferius, 32.4; 86.11, 17
infinitum, 36.9 (bis)
infinitus, 26.3; 68.3
infrascribi, 48.5
ingenium, 86.22
inimicari, 58.7
inquirere, 56.4
instrumentum, 36.10
insurgere, 32.12; 64.8; 68.4
intelligere, 34.4; intelligi, 32.4; 84.2
intendere, 26.5 (bis); 28.10, 13; 32.13, 15; 80.12; 82.2, 12; 86.4, 8, 13, 20; intendi, 60.7
intentio, 62.3, 4
interponere, 62.10; 64.7
interpretatio, 30.2
inveniri, 28.2; 52.9; 72.3
inventor, 26.3
inventum, 26.2, 3
investigatio, 56.1
la, 34.6
laborare, 26.6

largus, 28.8
linea, 78.5
locus, 36.19 (bis); 70.3; 72.1, 8; 74.11; 80.9, 11, 12; 82.2; 86.4, 8, 12, 19
maior, 44.3, 7; 48.4; 52.6, 9, 12, 15; 54.1 (bis), 4, 5; 56.1; 64.4; 76.16; 80.1, 7, 8, 13; 82.3, 4, 5; 86.3, 5, 7, 9, 18; *v.* octava maior, quinta maior, semitonium maius, sexta maior, tercia maior
maioritas, 44.4; 80.5; 86.3, 10, 14, 21
manus, 36.11, 13, 14, 16, 19
maximus, 64.1; *v.* octava maxima
medius, 40.2
mentio, 44.3
mi, 34.5; 36.15; 62.14; 70.4 (bis); 76.2, 6, 7, 8
minimus, 94.2
minor, 44.3; 44.7, 8; 48.4; 52.8, 11, 14, 17; 54.2 (bis), 4, 6; 56.1; 62.1; 64.4; 76.16; 80.7, 9; 82.1, 3, 4, 5; 86.7, 18; *v.* octava minor, quinta minor, semitonium minus, sexta minor
minoritas, 44.4; 80.5; 86.5, 8, 12, 19
modernus, 26.8; 46.7
modus, 28.2, 8; 36.9; 58.6; 66.9; 68.1, 2; 76.10
mollis, 74.2, 3, 9, 12; 76.5, 7, 11; 86.6
motus, 60.6
mulceri, 60.1
musica, 44.12; 46.7; 62.12; *v.* ficta musica
musicalis, 34.5; 36.12, 13, 14, 16, 19
musicus, 56.2, 94.1
natura, 58.7; 60.2, 5; 64.9; 74.2
neccessarius, 32.15; 70.2
neccessitas, 72.1, 2; 74.1
nichil, 32.10; 72.2
nominari, 28.11, 15; 34.8; 58.4; 60.3
nona, 34.13; 36.4; 38.9
nota, 28.4; 78.3, 4, 6; nota contra notam, 28.2-3, 9-10, 13-14; 30.1, 3-4, 4
notabilis, 72.6
notare, 58.2; notari, 48.4
noticia, 30.7 (bis); 48.3; 78.8
nullus, 44.3, 4; 52.7; 58.5; 62.9, 11
numerari, 40.5; 44.12; 46.1, 6, 11; 48.3
numerus, 50.4, 5, 9, 11, 13, 15, 18, 19
obviare, 26.7
octava, 34.10, 12; 36.3, 8; 38.5; 42.4; 46.6, 10; 52.10, 13; 66.5 (bis); 78.10; octava maior, 46.4; 58.13; 60.12-13; 86.5, 9; octava maxima, 46.11; 48.2; 58.5; octava minor, 46.8-9; 58.5;
omnis, 32.4; 34.8, 11; 44.2; 52.1, 5, 6, 9, 12, 15; 54.8; 72.7; 86.21

operari, 76.10
oportet, 54.6; 60.1; 78.11; 80.4, 5
opportunus, 80.5
oppositus, 76.10 (bis)
opus, 74.5
opusculus, 26.4
ordinari, 62.6
ordinatio, 58.1
pars, 36.11, 13, 14, 16
perfectio, 82.9
perfectus, 42.2 (bis), 4, 5, 9; 44.12; 46.6; 52.18, 19; 58.12; 60.3, 11; 66.2, 8; 82.10, 12 (bis)
permanere, 56.5
persuasivus, 82.8
pertractari, 70.2
planus, *v.* cantus planus
plus, 28.2, 9
ponere, 62.14; 70.4; 74.3; 76.1; 84.12; poni, 66.8; 72.1, 2; 76.4, 5, 6; 78.1, 2, 10; 80.3; 82.4; 86.1, 2, 10, 15; 86.16, 18
positio, 28.10, 14; 70.3
pratica, 32.10
praticus, 56.3
precedere, 60.6
predecessor, 26.6; 34.8
preponi, 60.4
presupponere, 32.10
primus, 50.1; 58.3; 86.2, 16
procedere, 36.9
proferri, 32.3, 8
pronuntiari, 62.5
proportio, 44.13; 46.8
propositum, 56.2
proprius, 32.2; 58.2
provenire, 74.5; 82.7
quantitas, 50.1, 7, 11, 15, 19
quarta, 34.10; 36.1, 2, 5; 38.8; 40.1; 50.14, 16 (bis), 58.4
quarta decima, 36.2, 7; 38.9
quartus, 54.8; 62.7
quaternarius, 50.14, 19
quatuor, 46.2, 9; 52.17
quinarius, 50.18
quinque, 46.5
quinta, 34.10; 36.2, 6; 38.4; 42.3; 44.11; 50.18, 20; 52.7, 10; 66.4 (bis); 78.10; quinta maior, 44.10; 58.13; 60.12; quinta minor, 44.13; 58.4-5;
quinta decima, 36.3, 8; 38.5-6; 52.16
quintus, 62.13

ratio, 58.14; 62.1; 64.7; 76.3; 82.6, 8 (bis)
re, 34.5
recedere, 80.11
recessus, 80.10
recitari, 34.9
reddere, 34.4; 42.5, 9
reducere, 54.5; 78.12; 80.5
regula, 48.5; 50.1; 52.4; 54.3, 8; 58.2, 3, 11; 60.9; 62.7; 64.3
relinqui, 68.5
remanere, 50.7, 10, 15, 19
removi, 50.10, 14, 18-19
reperiri, 36.12, 15, 19; 44.1, 5, 6, 11; 50.3, 8, 12, 16, 20; 52.7, 10, 12, 14, 16; 54.9; 62.11; 66.9; 86.6, 15
reprobare, 26.8
res, 56.3, 4; 82.10
resonare, 38.3, 7
scientia, 32.11
scire, 38.1; 40.1; 66.2; 78.1; 80.8; sciri, 28.6; 32.1, 9, 12; 42.4; 44.1; 70.5; 72.3; 74.8; 76.9; 78.9-10
scribere, 26.1; 68.1; scribi, 28.3, 5; 30.4; 32.3, 8
scriptura, 68.4-5
scriptus, 32.2, 3, 7, 8
secunda, 34.9, 13; 36.4, 18; 38.8; 50.6, 8 (bis); 58.4, 11
secundus, 26.1; 36.18; 52.4; 86.17
semitonium, 44.9, 11, 14-15; 46.3, 4, 5, 10; 48.1; 50.2, 8, 9, 11, 13, 16, 17, 20, 21; 52.1, 8, 9, 11, 12, 14, 17, 19; 54.8-9; 56.1; 76.15-16; semitonium maius, 54.4, 7; 76.15; semitonium minus, 54.9
sentiri, 58.10
septima, 34.10; 36.2, 7; 38.8; 58.4
sequi, 32.5, 6; 54.5; 78.7; 86.5, 9, 14, 20
sex, 48.1
sexquialterus, 44.13
sexta, 34.10; 36.2, 6; 38.4; 42.6; 66.5; 80.3; 86.12, 13; sexta maior, 46.1-2, 86.7; sexta minor, 46.3; 86.3
sextus, 64.3
signum, 74.8, 10; 76.9 (bis), 15; 78.1, 6, 9, 11; 80.3; 82.4; 86.1
similis, 78.10
simplex, 56.3
sol, 34.6
solus, 28.3, 4, 5, 9, 13 (bis); 52.8, 11, 19; 56.2, 4
spacium, 78.5
spectare, 56.2
speculatio, 56.3
speculari, 86.22

subripi, 50.6
sufficere, 94.1
sumere, 28.1; 82.1; sumi, 28.3, 5, 7, 9, 12; 30.6 (bis); 44.5; 58.2
superior, 86.2, 6, 15, 17
supradici, 84.2
tangere, 26.7 (bis); 32.13, 14; tangi, 32.14
tenere, 40.3
tenor, 78.4
tercia, 34.10; 36.4, 19; 38.14; 42.6, 7; 50.10, 12 (bis); 54.3; 66.4; 80.2; tercia maior, 44.78; 86.18
tercia decima, 36.2, 6; 38.5; 42.7
tercius, 36.20; 60.9
terminus, 30.2
ternarius, 50.9, 15
theoricus, 56.2
tonus, 44.8, 9, 10, 14; 46.2, 4, 5, 9; 48.1; 50.2, 7, 9, 11, 13 (bis), 15, 16, 20, 21 (bis)
totalis, 62.12
tractatulus, 32.13
tres, 44.10; 46.3, 10; 50.17, 21; 52.15, 16
ultimus, 54.8; 64.3
undecima, 36.1, 5; 38.9
unicus, 28.3, 4, 5, 9, 13; 52.8, 11, 19
unisonus, 34.9, 11, 12; 36.3, 8, 10, 15, 17; 38.4; 42.3; 44.2; 52.6; 58.13; 60.12; 66.4; 86.20
unitas, 50.5, 6, 7, 10, 14, 19
unus, 28.13; 34.13 (bis); 36.1, 18; 44. 11; 46.2; 48.1; 50.5, 17, 21; 62.1, 4; 66.3
usitari, 58.6, 8
usitatus, 26.8; 30.8
ut, 34.5
uti, 72.8
valere, 34.11, 13
variari, 78.4
velocitas, 58.9
verbum, 50.5; 66.3; 74.1
verus, 28.16; 40.3
videre, 80.11; videri, 32.15; 58.8; 62.12; 70.1, 4
vigesima, 36.6
vigesima prima, 36.7
vigesima secunda, 36.7-8
vocalis, 32.2; 32.7, 8
vox, 34.3, 4, 5; 36.9, 11, 12, 13, 14, 17, 18; 58.10; 62.2; 70.3 (bis); 74.3, 11, 12; 76.2 (bis), 5, 6; 78.3; *v.* combinatio vocum

INDEX NOMINUM ET RERUM

Albertus Magnus, 6
Anonymous II, 77n.9, 81n.10
Antonius de Leno, 61n.2, 63n.6
Antonius Monachus ac Paduanus (=de Lydo?), 19
Aristotle, 26-27
Ars musice plane optima et perfecta, 22
Boethius, 4, 6, 39n.4, 41n.6
Burzio, Niccolo, 31n.1, 49n.10, 59n.1, 61n.2, 63n.3, 65n.7, 67n.8, 83n.11
Capella, Martianus, 6
Cassiodorus, 6, 41n.6
Ciconia, Johannes, 12-13
Consonance, perfect and imperfect, 42-43
Counterpoint: six rules of, 8, 58-69; defined, 28-33
Coussemaker edition of Prosdocimo's *Contrapunctus*, 22-23
Cum notum sit, 6n.5, 31n.2, 33n.3, 63n.3, 63n.5
De diminutione contrapuncti, 6n.5
del Lago, Giovanni, 6n.5
Egidius de Murino, 21
Engelbert of Admont, 6
Eubulides, 41n.6
Franco of Cologne, 33n.3
Gaffurio, Franchino, 49n.10, 61n.2, 63n.3, 83n.11
Gamut, medieval, 37-39n.3, 47-49n.10
Gerbert of Aurillac, 6
Goscalcus, 6n.5, 31n.2, 35n.2, 61n.2, 63n.3, 65n.7, 83n.11
Guido of Arezzo, 49n.10
Guilielmus Monachus, 61n.2, 63n.3, 65n.6, 65n.7, 67n.8
Hippasus, 41n.6
Hothby, Johannes, 61n.2, 63n.3, 65n.6, 65n.7
Hugh of St. Victor, 6
Intervals: defined, 34-35; enumerated, 34-37; Greek names of, 35n.2, 40-41, 44-47; consonant and dissonant, 38-43; major and minor, 44-49; numerical size of, 50-53; constitution of, 52-57
Introductio musice secundum magistrum de Garlandia, 49n.10
Isidore of Seville, 6, 7n.6
Jacques de Liège, 49n.10, 61n.2
Johannes de Grocheio, 81n.10

Johannes de Muris, 4, 6, 19, 21
Johannes de Sacrobosco, 5
Johannes Scottus Eriugena, 6
Jordanus de Nemore, 5
Legrense, Johannes (Johannes Gallicus Carthusiensis), 31n.2, 33n.3, 49n.10
Leonardo of Pisa (Fibonacci), 5
Macrobius, 41n.6
Manuscript sources of Prosdocimo's *Contrapunctus*, 14-22
Marchetto of Padua, 11n.7, 14, 18, 49n.10, 77n.9, 83n.11, 85-87n.13; his division of the whole tone, 8-9, 54-57, 91-93n.15; his chromatic signs, 9-11n.7, 86-95
Monochord, anonymous treatise on, 19
Musica ficta: use and misuse of, 10-13, 70-75; defined, 12, 70-73; signs of, 74-79, 94-95; in perfect consonances, 78-81; in imperfect consonances, 80-87
Nicholas of Cusa, 6
Nicomachus, 41n.6
Nota quod unisonus de ut, 6n.5
Odington, Walter, 49n.10
Oresme, Nicole, 6
Paccioli, Luca, 5
Pelacani, Biagio, 5
Peter of Abano, 7n.6
Petrus dictus palma ociosa, 35n.2, 59n.1, 61n.3, 65n.7, 71n.1, 73n.2, 81n.10, 83n.11
Philippe de Vitry, 71n.1, 71n.2
Plain chant, 32-33
Post octavam quintam, 6n.5, 18
Prosdocimo: life of, 1; treatises of, 2-5, 15-16, 17, 19, 21, 22; *Contrapunctus* of, 2, 3n.2, 7-13, 15, 17, 18, 21, 22; *Tractatus musice speculative* of, 2, 3n.2, 8, 11n.7, 16, 22, 41n.7, 55n.13, 55-57n.14, 75n.8, 91n.14; *Tractatus plane musice* of, 2, 3n.2, 10n.7, 15, 17, 22, 47-49n.10; influence of, 5; his revision of the *Contrapunctus*, 8-13; historical significance of, 13-14
Ptolemy, 41n.6
Quantity, discrete, 50-51
Quatuor principalia, 6n.5, 31n.1, 49n.10, 59n.1, 61n.2, 61-63n.3, 63n.4, 5, 65n.7
Quilibet affectans, 6n.5, 21, 35n.2, 61n.2, 63n.3, 65n.7, 83n.11
"Quot sunt iuncture manus? . . ," 21
Ramos de Pareia, Bartolomeo, 61n.2, 63n.3, 65n.7, 67n.8, 83n.11
Remi of Auxerre, 6
Richardus Normandus, 77n.9
Semitone, major, 54-55, 76-77
Signatures, 78-79

Spataro, Giovanni, 6n.5
Tinctoris, Johannes, 6n.5, 12n.9, 31n.1, 49n.10, 59n.1, 61n.2, 63n.3, 65n.6, 7, 73n.2, 3, 4
Ugolino of Orvieto, 5, 6n.5, 31n.1, 33n.3, 37n.3, 49n.10, 59n.1, 63n.3, 5, 6, 65n.7, 67n.8, 71n.1, 73n.2, 77n.9, 81n.10, 83n.11, 85-87n.13, 97-98